FOODS

THE INDIANS GAVE US

Ives Washburn books by Wilma P. Hays

THE APRICOT TREE
CIRCUS GIRL WITHOUT A NAME
NAUGHTY LITTLE PILGRIM
THE LONG BLOND WIG
PILGRIMS TO THE RESCUE

FOODS
THE INDIANS GAVE US

by

Wilma P. Hays

and

R. Vernon Hays

ILLUSTRATED BY TOM O'SULLIVAN

IVES WASHBURN, INC.

NEW YORK, N. Y.

FOODS THE INDIANS GAVE US

LIBRARY OF CONGRESS CATALOG CARD NUMBER: 72-83041
MANUFACTURED IN THE UNITED STATES OF AMERICA

FOURTH PRINTING, JUNE 1976

ISBN: 0-679-24025-X

$2.38

To the ancient Indians of the Americas
who
cultivated many of nature's most nutritious foods—
foods that were adopted by New World colonists and
passed along to us as part of our heritage.

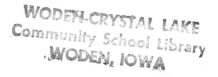

AUTHORS' NOTE

Whenever we travel we enjoy eating the foods that are native to the area we are visiting. We ask about their preparation and how they grow. Many of our most important foods came from the Indians of North and South America, and the Indians deserve recognition for this enormous contribution. Eating can be more fun when we know how these foods are planted, cultivated, and cooked.

Each chapter stresses one or more points: the importance of a stable food supply in the building of a stable civilization; the genius of Indian farmers in cultivating wild plants for food; and what modern man has done to improve these foods.

In the chapter on corn, for instance, we show that the search for knowledge never ends. There is still much to learn about early man and his foods, and we discover more every year.

We hope that readers will also learn the fun of home gardening and the enjoyment of cooking these natural, nutritious foods. A sampling of recipes is included in the hope our readers will experiment in "cooking the Indian way."

It is impossible to name each source we used in writing this book. Ideas and facts were checked in many books, magazines, and newspapers, and through personal interviews. We can list only a few major sources:

Foods America Gave the World by A. Hyatt Verrill, pub-

lished by L. C. Page and Co., 1937. *The Florida of the Incas* by
the Inca Garcilasco de la Vega, 1591, translated by Varner and
Varner, University of Texas Press, 1951. *The Gift is Rich* by
E. Russell Carter, Friendship Press, 1955. *National Geographic*,
November 1937 and May 1965; *The National Observer* and
Yankee, June 1970.

Pamphlets and correspondence from: Campbell Soup Company, Camden, New Jersey; The Dole Company, Hawaii; Hershey Foods Corporation, Hershey, Pennsylvania; Iowa State University, Ames, Iowa; National Peanut Council, Washington, D.C.;
Oklahoma Peanut Commission, Madill; Oklahoma State University, Stillwater, Oklahoma; Standard Brands Incorporated (Plant-
ers Peanuts); U. S. Department of Agriculture, Washington, D.C.;
University of Georgia College of Agriculture, Athens, Georgia;
University of Miami Institute of Marine Sciences, Miami, Florida.

We also wish to thank the public librarians in Venice, Florida;
Lincoln, Nebraska; and New Haven and Branford, Connecticut
who assisted us in obtaining books we needed for research.

Wilma P. Hays and
R. Vernon Hays
Venice, Florida

CONTENTS

FOODS

THE INDIANS GAVE US

❧ 1 ❧

HOW INDIAN FOODS
CAME TO US

Eighty percent of our present food plants were unknown to Europeans before 1492. Early Spanish explorers invaded the New World in search of silver and gold. Many were successful, but they also carried home a treasure of far greater value—native American plants, seeds, and roots. One year's crop of corn or potatoes is worth more to the world than all the gold and silver on all the galleons in all the great treasure fleets.

Today much of the world's population eats our native Indian foods—corn, potatoes, beans, squash, cocoa, tapioca, and fruits. Consider for a moment those ancient unsung heroes, the first men who dared eat lobsters or clams, or the first man who bit into a potato. Many foods were first developed and cultivated from wild plants and grasses by three great nations of Indians

—the Incas of Peru, the Mayas of Central America, and the Aztecs of Mexico. These highly civilized people had developed agriculture to a fine art long before Europeans came to the Americas.

The Incas have never been surpassed as agriculturists. Our most important American food plants originated with them. The Incas not only cultivated wild plants, they hybridized them (particularly maize) and grew plants in fields that were watered by vast irrigation systems. They terraced gardens to conserve soil, and they rotated crops. They also allowed fields to lie fallow to restore fertility.

The Incas could not have developed their powerful civilization if they had not ended the nomadic wandering of their many tribes and learned to grow foods. Agriculture must come first, for the key to the growth of any nation is "enough food to feed its people." Only then can men, women, and children spend their energy and talents developing better government, transportation, architecture, arts and crafts, and communication with each other and other nations.

The ancient Mayas and Aztecs had many of the same food plants as the Incas, but they developed different ways of growing them. The Mayas, in their wet jungles, did not turn the earth in a whole field. They chopped the weeds, then used digging sticks to make holes for the seeds. The Aztecs developed a slash-and-burn method that suited their land. They cleared the brush and trees with axes, then burned the brush for the ashes to fertilize their crops.

When the first European colonists came to the New World they found small, isolated North American tribes growing three important Indian food plants—maize, beans, and squash. Many North American Indians were basically hunters who planted only small garden patches. Some still used the digging stick.

Other tribes used crude wooden hoes to dig "hills" into which they dropped fish for fertilizer before planting corn seeds. Still other tribes, such as the Iroquois, had well-tended fields of corn and squash.

At a time when travel was so difficult, how did food plants, developed by the Incas, Mayas, and Aztecs, reach Indian tribes in both North and South America, from the Atlantic to the Pacific? How did seeds from ancient South American Indians reach the Indians of North America? There are several probable answers.

Most Indian tribes were nomadic—some because they enjoyed the adventure of wandering, others because they were driven by changes in climate and the constant search for food. For thousands of years small family groups had traveled farther and farther from their early homes. They carried seeds with them and planted crops whenever they stopped long enough for plants to mature.

The Incas were more than farmers—they had built a system of roads that made travel and trade possible. Indians from distant tribes came to the great Inca cities to exchange goods, and Inca merchants sent caravans long distances for the same purpose. Seeds were carried in bundle-packs on the backs of human cargo carriers who trotted hundreds of miles over narrow trails between tribal villages.

The early tribes of Peru used domesticated llamas, small cousins of the camel. Llamas made their way over mountains wherever a burro could find no footing. Llamas could travel for long periods without water. They could carry about a hundred pounds on their backs, their fleece was used for weaving cloth, and their hide for leather. They gave milk and their meat was good to eat.

Llamas could cross burning deserts, grazing on stunted plants that would kill a less adaptable beast. Just as the railroad opened up western United States to settlers, llamas provided a way for South American Indians to travel great distances over high mountain ranges and across arid deserts. And seeds went with them.

There was also a brisk sea trade, particularly among the ancient Mayas and Aztecs. Fleets of dugout canoes, some sixty feet long, plied the coastal waters. Indian seafarers visited isolated villages along both coasts and seeds were among the trade items they carried.

Also, over thousands of years, small groups of southern Indians migrated north—moving slowly, a few miles at a time. Along the way they merged with local tribes and shared their precious food seeds. North American Indians were wanderers, too. Modern archaeological diggings show that many tribes traveled great distances in spring, summer, and fall to social gatherings throughout what is now the United States. Artifacts uncovered in mounds on Cape Cod prove that tribes from the midwest and northwest gathered there for clam, oyster, and corn feasts. The remains of such feasts are also found along beaches as far south as Florida. Here the Indians dined on shrimp and fish. Each time the tribes gathered they traded or gave each other gifts of seed.

Fortunately for the settlers of Jamestown, the Pilgrims at Plymouth, and many others who followed, Indian corn, beans, and squash, had reached Virginia and New England before they did. The Indians traded seeds to the colonists, taught them how to plant, and showed them which seafoods to eat. Many colonists would not have survived their first harsh years in the New World without the foods the Indians gave them.

❧ 2 ❧

THE POTATO

1: *The Common White or Irish Potato*

A severe famine, following the failure of the potato crop in Ireland in 1845, dramatized the importance of potatoes to the Irish. People called them "Irish spuds," forgetting that both the common white potato and the sweet potato came from the Indians of South America.

Six thousand years ago pre-Incan Indians in the valleys of the Andes Mountains on the Pacific Coast of South America were cultivating potatoes. No one knows just when these early Indians learned that the tubers on the wild potato plant were safe to eat. The plant is a member of the nightshade family, which often bears poison berries above ground.

The skill of ancient Indians in developing better food plants from wild potatoes, corn, and beans kept them healthy and

6

strong. With plenty to eat, the Incas turned their energy and talents toward improving their lives.

By the time Columbus reached America, the Incas were a proud, efficient nation of some ten million people in a number of different tribes. The Incas were skilled in government as well as agriculture. Their architects planned and constructed thousands of miles of roads and irrigation canals. They built great temples of stone, bridges, and cities along two thousand miles of South America's west coast. Their ranks included skilled stonemasons, pottery makers, weavers of cloth, and craftsmen in gold and silver.

Then, between 1532 and 1537, Francisco Pizzaro, the Spanish conqueror, destroyed the Inca civilization. He slaughtered their leaders and more than eight million Indians. A few survivors escaped by hiding in forests and mountain caves. Gradually the temples, cities, aquaducts, canals, roads and bridges fell into ruin. Only one thing remained to the surviving Incans: their knowledge of agriculture. They still knew how to grow potatoes, maize, beans, and other plant foods. They were poor and scattered but they survived.

White and sweet potatoes are still one of the principal foods of their descendants. A far greater variety of potatoes is sold today in South America than in the United States. Indian farmers sell tubers in natural rainbow colors—pink, red, green, lavender, white, purple, and black. They sell tiny potatoes and giant potatoes, some weighing several pounds each. These potatoes are the same as those planted by Inca Indians thousands of years ago. No completely new variety has been developed since the great day of the Incas.

Pizzaro and his adventurers lived off the land in the New World. They learned to eat potatoes and they saw how potatoes were grown. Pizzaro took potatoes home with him to Spain and urged Spanish farmers to plant them. A few Spaniards did eat them, but most were afraid to eat any member of the nightshade family.

In 1560, when Spanish colonists settled in Florida, they brought potatoes along, for potatoes kept better than most fresh vegetables on a long sea voyage. Potatoes had returned to the New World, this time to the southeast coast of North America.

Not long after this, British adventurers raided Spain's Florida colonies. They found little worth taking except food, which they needed on their return voyages. They carried tubers back to England, where British farmers planted them to feed hogs and cattle. They didn't consider them fit for humans. Across the English Channel in France, Louis XVI soon recognized that potatoes could provide his country with an abundant new food. But most Frenchmen were as stubborn as the English about eating tubers, even though Louis promoted potatoes by wearing white sprays of potato blossoms in his lapel. He also ordered them served at dinner in the palace.

From England, potatoes were carried to Ireland. The Irish were either wiser or hungrier than other Europeans. They took to potatoes at once. Potatoes became a staple food throughout Ireland, and other Europeans soon thought of them as a native "Irish food."

Almost a hundred years after the Spanish had carried potatoes from the Indians of South America to Spain, English colonists carried them back across the Atlantic to Jamestown and Plymouth. But English colonists still didn't *eat* them, they fed them to their hogs! Many stoutly believed that potatoes were poisonous or caused leprosy and other diseases. Apparently they weren't overly concerned about their hogs.

Potatoes did not become an important food in the colonies of eastern North America until 1719, when Irish settlers in Lon-

donderry, New Hampshire, planted enough tubers to feed their families for an entire winter. This was news of the greatest interest to other colonies, for the early settlements were always short of food in winter.

Thus, after two hundred years during which this remarkable vegetable had traveled from South America to Spain, from Spain to Florida, from Florida to England and Ireland, and from Ireland back to the east coast of North America, the potato became a respectable—and popular—food in the American colonies.

For years the Indians of New England and Virginia had grown corn, squash, and beans, but they didn't have potatoes until they traded with the colonists. Then, for the first time, northeastern Indians began to grow potatoes that had been developed by their kinsmen in South America.

The cultivation of the potato spread slowly westward as white settlers pushed deeper into the wilderness. Although they are grown in most parts of the country, they became a major crop in the northern states and across Canada.

Idaho, with its high, cool climate and a soil that contains much volcanic ash, produces more potatoes than any other state. Maine comes next in total production, followed by California, Washington, New York, North Dakota, Minnesota, Oregon, and Wisconsin. The fifty states produce more than thirty *billion* bushels each year. This volume would equal the weight of the seven and a half million automobiles that are manufactured in the United States each year.

How are thirty billion bushels of potatoes used? A small percentage are used for starch, alcohol, and potato flour. Most of them are eaten in homes and restaurants: baked, boiled, fried, creamed, mashed, and as chips.

Americans like potato chips, which were invented in 1853 by

an American Indian chef in a restaurant in Saratoga Springs, New York. Two hundred million pounds of potatoes are made into chips each year and another sixty million pounds are processed into french fries, or are canned, or dehydrated into flakes.

As important as the potato is in the United States, it is even more important in Europe. For every *one* billion bushels produced in the fifty states, *nine* billion bushels are produced by Europeans. Potatoes are grown all over the world for they yield more pounds of food per acre than any other plant. If it weren't for this gift from Indians of the past millions would die of starvation today.

The planting and reproduction cycle of the white potato is unusual. A full-grown potato has "eyes," small depressions in its jacket. Sprouts grow from these eyes. If planted with care, each sprout will grow into a leafy vine—a plant that is about two feet high. Above ground, small white flowers bloom, then drop off. Small green berries sometimes form.

Under the soil, along the root-ends of the plant, new potatoes form. Within several months they grow from pin-head size to tubers that weigh as much as half a pound. Commercial growers prefer to sell smooth, unmarked potatoes, so they machine-spray them to control the bugs that attack the vines. Commercial potatoes are dug, cleaned, and sorted by complex machines. They are shipped to market at once or placed in cool, dark storage for later sale. A fully matured tuber will not produce sprouts until five or six weeks after the leafy vine dies, indicating that the potato is ready to eat. If it weren't for this natural timing, potatoes in the ground would sprout before the farmer could harvest them. Growers know that nature will allow them approximately forty days to dig, grade, and ship mature potatoes before the tubers are ruined by sprouting.

Potato growing is easy and satisfying for anyone who wants
to raise one of our best natural foods. If a potato is placed in a
dish of water it will sprout and grow a plant—but it will not
produce new potatoes. But anyone can grow a potato that will
produce, even in a small backyard. One good potato will produce enough seed for four plants. Simply cut it into four pieces,
making sure each section has at least one eye. Choose a sunny

place at the end of a flower bed or along a back fence. For four hills, spade an area of about eighteen inches by four or five feet. Smooth down the soil. Use a hoe to dig a ditch about six inches deep down the center of the plot. Place the four pieces of potato, eyes up, about a foot apart in the ditch. Cover them with two inches of soil.

The sprouts will soon show above ground. When they do, fill in the ditch and let Mother Nature and the potatoes do most of the work. Potatoes need water but not too much water. If bugs nibble at your vines, show no mercy—pick them off and destroy them.

After several months, when the vines die down, dig the potatoes. There should be about three good-sized potatoes under each plant—twelve tubers in all. That's enough to start forty-eight plants, or enough to provide a good dinner for a big family. Many Americans believe that a traditional Fourth of July dinner should include new potatoes cooked with new peas.

This backyard planting is little different from potato growing thousands of years ago in what is now Peru and Chile. The wild tubers that had been found by Indians were small, scaly, and warty. They tasted like soft wood pulp. Wild potatoes are the same today. Pre-Incan Indians selected only the best wild tubers for planting near their homes. They later learned to hybridize plants by taking pollen from the best vines to fertilize the blossoms on other plants. Gradually, over the years, they developed the excellent potatoes that the world consumes by the billions of bushels today.

2: *The Sweet Potato*

The word potato comes from one of the Incan words for sweet potato—*batata*. Indians called the common white potato *papa*. The Spanish lumped all tubers together, calling them all *batatas*. The British pronounced it "potato."

Although ancient Indians developed many varieties of sweet and white potatoes from wild plants, the two are not closely related. A sweet potato vine resembles a morning glory vine and its small trumpet-shaped flowers look like morning glory blossoms. Sweet potato tubers grow underground, but not at the end of root branches as white tubers do. Sweet potato roots simply grow larger until they become tubers. These swollen roots grow in many sizes and shapes—round, long, thin, gnarled, and fat. The meat of most varieties is golden brown when cooked, has a sweet, nutty flavor, and packs more energy value, pound for pound, than the white potato. Many Americans feel that they should have sweet potatoes glazed with honey, brown sugar, or cranberry, for Thanksgiving dinner.

The sweet potato needs a more exact climatic condition than the white to thrive. It requires a moist warm climate, a growing season of at least four months, and light, sandy loam soil. This may account for the fact that the United States produces only one-tenth as many pounds of sweet potatoes as it does white. Among the fifty states, Louisiana produces the most, followed by North Carolina, Virginia, Texas, Georgia, South Carolina, and Maryland.

A sweet potato will sprout in a sunny windowsill if a tuber is placed in a dish with an inch or two of water. The climbing vine makes a pretty indoor plant. It will produce tubers if it is transplanted outside in the right soil and temperature. In southern states, where sweet potatoes are grown commercially, nurseries sell vines that have already sprouted and are ready to be planted. These are set in hills or rows about two feet apart. They require a longer time to make tubers than white potatoes do.

The first recorded planting of sweet potatoes by British colonists was in Virginia in 1617, about ten years after the founding
of Jamestown. Although Englishmen would shun white potatoes
for another hundred years, they ate sweet potatoes as soon as
they learned about them. Other Europeans were just as strange.

Sweet potatoes were also carried from South America to
Spain. From Spain they traveled to Italy, Belgium, Germany,
and England. Englishmen were eating sweet potatoes before Sir
John Hawkins and other English marauders carried the first
white tubers home from Florida.

Historians know that both Pizzaro and Columbus took sweet
potatoes back to Spain, yet there is a mystery as to where men
first developed them. Unlike white wild potatoes, which have

been found growing in the Andes, no wild sweet potato plant has ever been discovered. Their origin is unknown. Most authorities believe they were cultivated by the same pre-Columbian Indians that developed white potatoes. The Incas were certainly growing them in great varieties when the first white men reached America. Oddly enough, the first white men who arrived in New Zealand also found the natives growing and eating sweet potatoes. The Maoris of New Zealand lived thousands of miles from the coast of South America. How did the sweet potato cross the Pacific Ocean from Peru? Did the Maoris develop the vine themselves, or did sweet potato tubers drift on ocean currents like that hardy traveler, the coconut. This seems unlikely, for sweet potato tubers are very perishable and are easily bruised. When bruised, they rot; and unlike white potatoes they do not have a rest period after they mature—they sprout immediately. A more plausible explanation would be that the Maoris may have visited South America in their long, dugout canoes and carried sweet potatoes back across the Pacific as provisions. One thing is certain: the Maori word for sweet potato is the same as the word used by the Incas.

If the Polynesians were superior seamen, the Incas were not to be surpassed in their principal field of endeavor—agriculture. They gathered wild plants and developed them by cultivation and by hybridization. They rotated crops. They terraced their gardens and watered their fields with irrigation canals. They fertilized with compost, bird droppings called *guano,* and llama manure. They used wooden hoes and spades that were tipped with stone and curved wooden plows. Incan farmers trampled seeds into the soil with their feet and crumbled clods of earth with their hands or stones. Their work was hard but they raised primitive agriculture to a fine and valuable art.

❧ 3 ❧

THE PEANUT

Peanuts came to the United States with black men, and a black scientist, Dr. George Washington Carver, showed us two hundred ways to use them. Yet peanuts are another gift from the Indians, for they originated in the wilds of Brazil, Uraguay, and Paraguay.

The peanut is probably the nearest perfect food-producing plant. The "mighty peanut" has been described as "Nature's Food Masterpiece."

North Americans call it the peanut. South Americans call it *mani* (*mah-nee*), the "earth seed." In Europe and some other parts of the world, it is the "ground nut" or "ground pea."

The peanut is not really a nut at all; it belongs to the leguminous bean and pea family. Its leaves and blossoms look much like pea vines. But beans and peas produce their food pods on vines above ground, while peanuts form underground.

When the yellow blossoms fade on a peanut vine, they leave sharp-pointed pegs. In a few days the pegged branches turn downward, closer to the earth. When a peg touches the ground it drills into the soil, where it grows into a pod that is filled with peanut kernels.

If the soil is too hard or rocky, the pegs can't penetrate, and will shrivel and die. Yet somehow peanuts survived as wild plants until pre-Incan farmers developed and cultivated them.

Peanuts, like potatoes, were unknown in other parts of the world until the Spanish reached South America. Pods of peanuts have been found with Indian mummies in tombs that are three thousand years old. Some kept so well in the dry, closed tombs that they can be seen today in Peruvian museums. These ancient peanuts look much like our basic varieties. Incans, Mayans, and Aztecs decorated handmade pottery bowls with pictures of peanut pods and plants. Indian pottery makers scratched scenes in the smooth brown clay before it baked hard in the hot sun and some of those pictures show how peanuts were used. Indians ate them roasted as we do today or they pounded them into a brown paste—pre-Columbian peanut butter! They extracted peanut oil by pounding the kernels between stones, and they used the meal-pulp residue to make flat cakes. They even used cracked nuts in a candy made of boiled sugar or honey. Ancient Indians played games that were much like football and handball, and they may have eaten peanuts while they rooted for the home team, scattering peanut shells over their grassy bleachers.

The cultivation of peanuts spread northward for more than a thousand years—from South to Central America, on to Mexico, and through the islands of the West Indies.

Spanish treasure-seekers carried peanuts back to Spain and Portuguese traders took them from Spain to Portugal and to Af-

rica. Peanuts thrived in Africa. The peanut plant requires a
warm—or hot—climate. They grow best in sandy loam soil, and
where it rains once a week. The plants do not die if it is dry for
weeks; they simply lie dormant, waiting for rain. When it does
rain, peanut plants spring back to life and produce a bumper
crop.

Africa offered the right growing conditions and the cultivation of peanuts quickly spread across the continent. The natives
along the coastal areas were delighted to find a food that would
keep for many months with little spoilage. This quality of the
peanut was the reason for its strange odyssey back to the Western Hemisphere. Peanuts were carried aboard slave ships to
feed the captive blacks on the long voyage to the West Indies
and America. Ship captains sold leftover peanuts to plantation
owners in the southern states so the slaves could raise their own
food. The blacks planted peanuts in small patches around their
cabins. They fed them to the hogs, and they roasted them for
themselves. Black children sometimes shared peanuts with
white plantation children, so peanuts slipped in the back doors
of the big white owners' houses. Plantation owners recognized a
good thing when they saw it; here was a food that satisfied all
—their slaves, their hogs, and their children. Before long, larger
and larger fields were given over to the cultivation of peanuts.

Peanuts were scarcely known in the north when the War Between the States began in 1860. Southern soldiers carried peanuts with them on campaigns, and five years later, when the
war ended, most Northern soldiers had acquired a taste for peanuts. When they were home again, they tried to buy them in
Northern markets, but peanuts were still a rarity north of the
Mason and Dixon Line. Southern growers soon remedied that.
A lost war had expanded the peanut market, but nearly half a
century would pass before peanuts would become a popular

food for humans throughout the United States. Then, in the early 1900s, circus promotors such as P. T. Barnum, started to sell roasted peanuts in the shell under the big tops. About the same time, baseball became a popular national sport and five-cent bags of peanuts were hawked through the stands. The lowly peanut had come into its own. Tons of peanut shells soon littered grandstands and stadiums—so many that a San Francisco baseball manager banned them from his ball park. His customers rebelled and his team played its next game before row after row of empty seats. In desperation he advertised in local newspapers: "PLEASE COME BACK! FREE PEANUTS FOR EVERYONE!" The peanut hasn't been challenged since.

Today the United States produces a million tons of peanuts each year. The government limits the number of acres that can be planted. This prevents overproduction and assures the farmer a fair price for his crop.

Peanuts thrive in three areas of the United States—the Southeast, the Deep South, and the West. A large-kernel species called the *Virginia* grows well in that state, as well as in North Carolina and part of South Carolina. The *Runner* variety also flourishes there. This area supplies one-fourth of the entire peanut crop of the United States.

Half of the nation's peanut crop is grown in Georgia, Alabama, Florida, Mississippi, and the southern part of South Carolina. These are *Spanish* or *Red-skins,* a round peanut about the size of a pencil eraser. *Runners* and some *Virginias* are also grown in these states. Most of these peanuts go to market as "salted peanuts" or they are made into peanut butter.

Spanish peanuts also grow well in the irrigated fields of the West and Southwest—Oklahoma, Texas, Louisiana, Arkansas, Arizona, New Mexico, and California.

Half of the annual peanut crop is made into peanut butter,

which was first produced in 1890. A St. Louis physician recognized that peanuts were an excellent food. He experimented and made a peanut paste or "butter," which he prescribed for patients who couldn't eat other high-protein foods. A pound of peanut butter has as much food energy as a thick steak, or four quarts of milk, or thirty-two eggs. A thickly spread peanut butter sandwich has as much protein as two eggs.

About the time the St. Louis doctor was showing his patients how to make a mashed peanut spread at home, a young black man named George Washington Carver was graduated from Iowa State College. Born of slave parents in Missouri, Carver studied to be a scientist before he went on to teach at Tuskegee Institute in Alabama. Throughout his long life he experimented to find ways to use peanuts, the "goober peas" that had grown so profusely around the shacks of poor men when Carver had been a child.

Armed with the knowledge and authority of a scientist, Carver persuaded Southern farmers to plant peanuts in fields that were worn out from producing cotton every year. He showed them that peanut plants enriched the soil, for their roots sprouted small knobs of nitrogen that fertilized the earth. As more and more farmers grew more and more peanuts, Carver knew they had to create a larger market for the excess crop. He began research to find new uses for peanuts, not only the kernels, but for the entire plant. By the time he died, in 1943, Carver had spent fifty years studying peanuts and had listed over two hundred uses for this valuable plant. Among the most important of these was peanut oil, which is used in vegetable shortening and margarine, and salad and cooking oils.

George Washington Carver, with other scientists and the United States Department of Agriculture, found that peanuts not only enrich the soil and provide food pods, but the vines

themselves are good feed for livestock. Peanut hulls are used as cattle feed and fertilizer, so no part of the plant is lost.

A peanut grower saves his best raw peanuts as seed for his next crop. These "seeds" are planted three to four inches apart, two to three inches deep in the soil. The width between the rows varies according to the kind of peanuts grown. The sandy, freshly plowed soil is then leveled, covering the seed.

Peanuts need at least a five-month growing season, so they are usually planted in April or early May. As soon as the seed sprouts, the grower cultivates to keep the weeds down and the soil loose. His principal enemies at this point are aphids, borers, leaf blight, soil fungus, and nematodes. The grower must be expert in knowing just when to harvest his crop. If he digs too soon, the peanuts will shrivel. If he waits too long, they may mold or turn dark and lose their flavor. He solves the problem by testing.

As harvest time nears, the farmer digs sample peanuts in various parts of the field. When the samples show that the lining inside the shell is beginning to turn brown, he knows it is time to harvest. (*Virginia* peanuts do not turn brown. They are harvested about 140 days after planting.)

A peanut harvesting machine cuts into the soil below the pods, lifts the vines, roots, and pods and knocks off the soil. The vines are then dropped onto the ground, root-side up, so the pods will dry quickly. Several days later a combine picks up the dried vines and strips off the pods. The vines are left on the ground. The pods are carried to a drying station, where 95 percent of the moisture is removed by forced air, and the peanuts are inspected for quality. The grower then bales the vines for cattle feed, and plows under the roots for fertilizer. Nothing is wasted. It is easy to see why the peanut is called "the perfect plant."

Peanuts are processed by versatile machines that wash them, bleach them, sort them for size, split open their shells, remove their skins, and roast and salt their kernels. There are even machines that split the kernels, remove the heart or germ, press out the oil, and grind the peanuts for peanut butter. The eating is left to human beings.

Almost half the weight of peanuts is oil. If the oil is removed, the hard flat cake that is left can be fed to cattle or used for fertilizer.

The cultivation and processing of peanuts has changed greatly over the years, more than for any other Indian food plant, but it is still possible for anyone who lives in the "peanut belt"—those states with a five-month frost-free growing season —to grow peanuts the way the Indians did.

To do this, buy raw untreated peanuts through a seed catalog. Spade a small patch of soil that is in the sun all day. A patch that is eighteen inches wide and six feet long is large enough for a respectable peanut patch. Rake the soil until it is smooth, then make a ditch down the center, about two and a half inches deep. Plant single peanut kernels three inches apart along the ditch and cover to the level of the bed. Pat the soil over each seed with your hand and rake it lightly. The peanuts will sprout in about a week.

There is little to do then except to keep the weeds down and the bugs off. In October, dig them carefully, turning the vines over to expose the roots. After a few days, snip off the vines and hang the roots and peanut pods indoors to dry. When they are dry, shake off the soil and remove the pods. Your homegrown peanuts are now ready for roasting and salting. Shell the peanuts and spread a single layer of kernels in a shallow pan. Roast them in an oven at 300-degrees for thirty-five to forty minutes, then sprinkle them with salt. Butter or margarine can be added while they are hot, about one teaspoon to a cup of peanuts.

Although the United States grows only one-fifteenth of the world's total peanut production, this country leads all other na-

tions in finding new ways to use this versatile plant as food.
Strange as it seems, many nations in a protein-starved world are
slow to recognize the value of the lowly peanut, another of our
gifts from the Indians.

❧ 4 ❧

BEANS

Europeans knew nothing about beans when Columbus landed in the New World, yet Indians from Chile to Canada were growing many varieties, including kidney, pea or navy, limas, and scarlet runners. Ancient Peruvian pottery pictures Indians holding beans in one hand and corn in the other. Almost every variety of edible bean grown today has been found in ancient Incan graves.

These dry beans and pottery are between three and four thousand years old. We know that pre-Columbian Indians grew beans, but we don't know where any of the many varieties of wild plants were first developed. It is possible that Indians in both North and South America developed their own varieties from different wild bean plants.

Although it was almost four hundred years after the "discovery" of peanuts in America before they became an important crop, three hundred years before Europeans decided that potatoes were fit to eat, and three hundred and seventy-five years before tomatoes became popular, beans earned instant acceptance all over the world. Beans filled a great need for many hungry people. They were easy to grow and quick to mature, and they were rich in proteins—a cheap, nourishing substitute for meat. Dried beans kept well, even for years, and they could be stored in a comparatively small space.

Sailors, tired of the rotting salt pork and dry corn meal that had been their main diet, welcomed dry beans on long voyages. Slavers filled their storage bins with beans to feed their human cargo long before peanuts were used on those ships. Explorers recognized their value and carried enough beans to last months or years, and the "desert rats" who prospected for gold and silver in the American West carried heavy bags of beans on their burros. Lumbermen, isolated for months in the deep woods, ate great bowls of beans, following the tradition of pioneers, trappers, hunters, and whole armies of soldiers who depended on beans as a staple food. It is doubtful if any of them knew—or cared—that they were eating "Indian food."

Atlantic Coast tribes were growing bumper crops of beans, corn, pumpkins, and squash in the same fields when Plymouth and Jamestown were founded. They prepared the earth and planted their crops with the same type of pointed sticks and sharp stones that were used by ancient southern Indians.

Primitive as their methods were, early Indian farmers developed two main types of bean plants. One was the low-growing "bush" bean. The other climbed vine-like, and was called "pole" bean.

There are many colors, shapes, and sizes of these two common types of beans. Those most often grown in the United States are pinto, navy or pea bean, yellow-eye, black-eye, kidney, and lima. The "aristocrat of all the bean family" is the lima, named for Lima, Peru, where the Spanish first found them.

The Incans called limas *Purutu,* meaning "little dove," since its blossoms resembled doves on the wing. Limas still grow wild in Guatemala, where they probably originated. Primitive plants can be found along the old Indian trade routes from Peru, where the Incans improved them, to many other parts of South and North America. When the colonists of Plymouth and Jamestown reached the New World, they found limas among the beans being grown by the Indians. California and the Eastern and Gulf states produce about sixty million pounds of the large, thin, cream-colored beans each year.

Kidney, navy, and yellow-eye beans are believed to have originated in Central America, where they were cultivated even before the limas. These "common" beans can be grown almost anywhere that has enough moisture and no frost for about two months. Common beans grow to maturity well into the Canadian Provinces.

Michigan, California, Colorado, Idaho, New York, Oregon, and Wisconsin produce great quantities of all kinds of dry, and snap or green string beans. The government limits the number of acres planted, but Americans grow all the beans they need— about seven pounds per person each year. The United States annually exports twenty-five million dollars worth of beans.

Green beans—the snap or string bean, and the green shell bean—are picked while the pods are young and tender. String beans are cooked whole, pod and all. They are *snapped* into pieces or the pods are sliced lengthwise into thin strips— "French style." Green *shell* beans are beans that are allowed to mature to full size, then shelled out of the pod before they harden.

A "dry" bean is any bean pod that has ripened until the beans

are hard and dry. Some of the more popular recipes for cooking
dry beans were passed down to us by Indian women. Indians of
different tribes prepared one of these dishes in much the same
way, and called it by related names—*squaquaquatush, misqua-
tash,* or *misichqustash.* Americans call it succotash and prepare
it the same old way—a mixture of lima or other shell beans and
whole kernels of green corn, cooked together. Indian women
sometimes added pemmican, the dried meat of wild deer or buffalo pounded into a powder. The starches in corn and the pro-

tein and carbohydrates in beans provided a very healthy diet. Indians planted corn and beans together, using a sharp stick to make a small hole or "hill" in the soil. Two or three kernels of corn were planted in the hill. Beans were planted around each hill. As the plants grew, the bean vines climbed the stalks of corn. At harvest time Indian women walked down the rows, filling baskets with ears of corn and pods of ripe beans—a ready-mixed succotash.

Early Mexican Indians preferred their beans plain. Beans were seldom mixed with corn. Black beans were ground with a stone and made into a paste. This paste was patted into flat cakes called *frijoles* (*free-ho-lays*), then baked on hot stones. The cakes were rolled and dipped in chili pepper sauce. Mexican Indians still do this today. *Frijoles* are also popular north of the border in Southwestern United States.

Indian women of the New England tribes were skillful at baking beans. Massachusetts settlers borrowed the recipe and called it "Boston Baked Beans." As delicious as Boston beans are, many people believe that Maine's "bean-hole" method is even better. Indian squaws dug a hole in the ground that was large enough to hold a pot. The hole was lined with stones and a hardwood fire was burned in the pit. The fire was kept going for hours until the stones were hot and the fire had burned down to red coals. A covered pottery pot or iron kettle, filled with prepared beans, was lowered into the pit. The pot was then covered with fresh seaweed, green hay, or leaves. A wet blanket or animal skin was placed over the pit. The beans baked slowly all night. Hot, delicious beans headed the menu the next day.

Beans are an ideal vegetable for a small garden. Beans sprout and mature quickly, and the plant fertilizes and restores the soil. Like all members of the "pea" family, including peanuts,

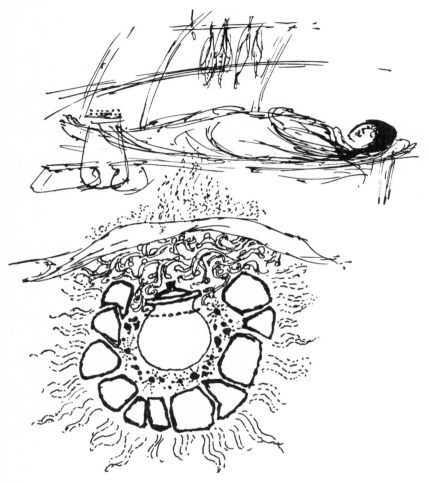

bean plants take nitrogen from the air and convert it into ni-
trates in the soil.

Seed beans are sold in packages in seed stores and in many
supermarkets. They can be planted in almost any small plot.
Bush beans are planted in "hills" or in rows, depending on the

type. Climbing, or "pole," beans should be planted Indian-style in hills. Unless they have cornstalks to climb, the gardener should provide poles or sticks, each about six feet long. Several seed beans are planted in a circle around each pole. The hills should be two feet apart. Tender green beans—string or snap— are ready to eat in about two months. If the pods mature a little longer, some beans may be shelled for cooking. Those beans that are left on the vine to dry and brown can be kept all winter.

Early Indians produced a satisfying variety of beans, and an even more satisfying variety of recipes for cooking them. Modern man has found few ways to improve on either technique.

❧ 5 ☙

TOMATOES

On a late summer day in 1820, Robert Gibbon Johnson of Salem, New Jersey, announced he would stand on the courthouse steps and publicly eat a tomato. Most people shook their heads—the man was mad; everyone *knew* tomatoes were poisonous!

But Robert Johnson wasn't so mad after all; he had eaten tomatoes in many parts of the world—and he *liked* them. The good people of Salem gaped while he ate one tomato, then another, and finally a small basketful. They waited, expecting him to drop dead. When he walked down the steps and drove away in his carriage, he left behind a group of converts to the glory of the tomato.

Indians in South and Central America were eating tomatoes thousands of years before Robert Johnson ever heard of them. Indian tribes in what is now Peru, Ecuador, and Bolivia found

tomatoes growing wild. Some tomato vines, fifty or more feet long, climbed trees; other bushes sprawled on the ground. One shrub-like tree tomato in Peru produced fruits that looked like yellow cherries.

Pottery vases found in pre-Incan Indian excavations in Peru have bases that are shaped like tomatoes. Carbon tests show this clay pottery to be many thousands of years old.

Tomato seeds are light and easy to carry, so tomatoes spread from tribe to tribe, as far north as modern Mexico. Spanish conquistadors found large fields of a fruit the Indians called "tomat'l" in this region. The Aztec taught the Spanish many ways to prepare tomatoes—raw or cooked or mixed with sweet red and green chili peppers.

The Spaniards carried tomato seeds home and planted the first tomatoes that were grown outside the New World. Tomatoes flourished in Spain's warm sunny climate, and varied in color—yellow, red, white, and purple. Whatever their color, the people of Spain liked their taste and invented many new ways to cook them. American tomato plants were soon grown all over Europe. Records show that as early as 1544 Italians fried tomatoes quickly in oil with salt and pepper.

Tomatoes do belong to the poisonous nightshade family—but so do white potatoes and chili peppers. Many Europeans grew them but few would eat them. The English and French grew tomatoes as decorative or ornamental plants. The yellow and red fruits were conversation pieces in their homes, but tomatoes were never served on their tables.

The French called the tomato *pomme d'amour* or "love apple." It could be admired and fondled but never eaten. Others called it "wolf peach," believing that it looked as delicious as ripe peach but was as dangerous as a wolf.

It was almost four hundred years before the widespread prejudice against eating tomatoes was overcome. Spanish and French settlers in Louisiana were among the first to eat tomatoes in the United States. They grew them in small patches along the banks of the bayous, as they still do today. By 1812 the Louisiana families were eating tomatoes fresh and in combination with chicken, fish, and rice. The delicious Creole dishes that were created by these settlers couldn't be prepared without tomatoes.

But old fears die hard, and the people who lived in the North

and East were among the last to accept the tomato as an edible fruit. Although it is true that Thomas Jefferson grew "tamatas" in his Virginia garden as early as 1781, and recorded them in his journal in 1809 as "a type of Spanish cantaloupe," he did *not* say that he ate them. At that time, seed catalogs listed tomatoes as "annual ornamental flowers."

After the Civil War, more people in the United States accepted tomatoes as a food. By 1892 there was a large demand for them. Growers experimented to grow larger, better-tasting tomatoes. They also thought that tomatoes would sell better if they were listed as a vegetable and they petitioned the United States Supreme Court, which ruled in 1893 that the tomato was a vegetable. Although botanically it is a fruit, it is found in markets with potatoes and beans.

Research and experiments have produced remarkable changes in tomatoes. Agricultural colleges and research farms have improved it in many ways. A tomato plant today has a stronger stem and a better root stock. Its fruit is a uniform bright red. The skin rarely cracks. The flesh is almost solid, with few seeds, and the flavor is better.

Until recently, all tomato plants had both green and ripe fruit on the vine at the same time, since each tomato ripened at a different rate. Tomatoes had to be picked by hand, a slow process. Growers worked to develop a plant or vine whose fruits would all ripen at the same time. Such a plant has been developed. This new tomato plant bloomed profusely only once, so all its tomatoes grew and ripened together.

In the United States, 400,000 acres of tomato plants are harvested annually for juice, catsup, sauce, and paste. This is sixty-five pounds of tomatoes for every man, woman, and child in the country.

California produces six times as many tons of tomatoes as does any other state. Ohio is second, followed by Florida, New Jersey, Indiana, Pennsylvania, Illinois, New York, and Michigan.

An additional 225,000 acres produce a million tons of tomatoes that are sold "fresh." These tomatoes are not picked by machines. Growers who supply fresh tomatoes daily prefer the usual tomato plants that blossom all season and ripen a few at a time. They are picked by hand each day, often by migrant workers who also harvest other perishable crops, such as beans, peas, cucumbers, and melons. Migrant workers and their families follow the growing seasons and harvests across the face of America. Whole families pick in the fields, and then they move on. Their lives have little security, for their livelihood depends on each new crop.

Fresh tomatoes can be bought all year long in every state. During the winter tomatoes are grown in open fields in Florida, Texas, Mexico, and the Virgin Islands. In the northern states and Canada, they are grown in greenhouses or during the shorter growing season.

Home gardeners, like truck farmers and nurserymen, prefer tomato plants that blossom and ripen all season. Tomatoes grow easily from seed, but most home gardeners buy seedling plants, and the sale of seedlings has become a big business in some parts of the country.

In Georgia, for example, some six thousand acres are planted with tomato seeds each year. About a hundred thousand seedlings are grown on each acre. The seedlings are dug up by hand when they are three to eight inches high. They are wrapped in wet moss and shipped to northern states and Canada, where they are set out in gardens as soon as the danger from frost is past. Tomato plants should be set about eighteen to twenty-four inches apart where there is full sunlight all day.

Some home gardeners let their vines spread over the ground, while others tie the plants to stakes that are about six feet high. A half-dozen plants will produce an ample supply of tomatoes for an average family until frost kills the vines. Tomatoes can be grown in hampers such as empty fruit baskets, but plastic or metal cans, about the five-gallon size, can also be used. If cans are used, three or four holes should be punched a few inches from the bottom to allow excess water to drain. The can or hamper should be filled with wood chips, shavings, or sawdust. One tomato plant is set in each container. The woodchips are moistened each day with a solution of fertilizer and water. This is called hydroponic gardening.

All nurseries sell liquid fertilizer. Usually one-half teaspoon to a gallon of water is used. During its first three weeks, each plant requires about a quart of the water-fertilizer solution daily. After that it will wilt if it doesn't get a gallon of the water solution each day.

When the plants are twelve to fourteen inches high and need support, a six-foot wood or metal stake is used to support the main stem which is tied to the stake with strips of cloth. A "hamper" tomato plant will bear as well as a plant that is grown in the ground, but, either way, tomato plants need plenty of sun.

⋊ 6 ⋉

THE PINEAPPLE

An unsung hero in this story is the first South American Indian who had the temerity to sample the fruit of the pineapple.

It is time to rectify this oversight.

The pineapple, for all its virtues, is an unlovely plant—a sort of porcupine fruit. Sharp spines form its crown and larger spines cover its cone-shaped stem, all the way to the ground. Our unsung Indian hero was either very curious or very hungry—or both, for the pineapple plant did little to instill confidence that under those spines was a good thing to eat.

Perhaps as long ago as 4000 B.C., South American Indians recognized this strange, armored fruit as edible. Pre-Incan pottery makers have left proof that pineapples were cultivated—and eaten—that long ago. Pictures on ancient pots show us that the cultivation of the pineapples began almost as early as the first primitive farming of the potato, the bean, the squash, and per-

4

haps even maize. We enjoy the results, but it is too bad these talented agriculturalists had no written language. Our unsung hero must remain unsung and we can only guess who and what he was.

From the evidence, it seems likely that pineapples were first cultivated in Brazil or Central America, where wild fruit can still be found. These wild pineapple plants are woody and full of seeds, much as the Indians must have found them.

On his second voyage to the West Indies, Columbus observed Indians growing a delicious fruit in fields on the island of Guadeloupe. By careful selection and cultivation, they had produced a much larger and sweeter fruit than the wild plants. Those forbidding spines were still very much a part of the plant.

Spaniards who followed Columbus to the West Indies found the Carib Indians growing these fruits, which the Indians called *anana*. The Spanish thought *anana* looked like a pine cone, so they called it *pina*. The English later added "apple" to "pine" and the fruit has since been known as pineapple.

Spanish explorers loaded the fruit aboard their ships, but it spoiled on the long voyage to Spain. They liked pineapples, so they tried again and again. On later voyages, they returned from the West Indies with cargoes of slips, suckers, and crowns from the plants.

They had learned from the Indians how to plant and cultivate the pineapple. Soon fields of pineapples were growing in warm and sunny southern Spain. Europeans loved pineapple and its use spread rapidly to England, France, and Holland, where it was grown in heated greenhouses. Within a short time Portugese and Spanish sailors had carried slips, suckers, and crowns of the plant to all parts of the tropical world.

The Spaniards learned from the Indians two additional uses for the pineapple plant—one lethal, one friendly. The conquer-

ing Spaniards learned the former the hard way. The Indians of the New World used the juice of decaying pineapple to poison the tips of their arrows, and more than one Spaniard found that the price of conquest comes high.

The second use of the pineapple was more gratifying. It pleased the Spaniards so much they adopted the custom as their own. The Indians, if they were feeling friendly, hung the crowns of pineapple at the entrances to their thatched huts as an invitation for all to enter. The Spanish introduced the custom to Spain and it soon spread all over Europe.

The British brought the idea to North Carolina, Virginia, and New England as the colonies were settled there. It soon became the custom to carve pineapples on doorways, gate posts, even on a furniture, as a symbol of friendship and hospitality. Craftsmen of early Virginia produced the symbol in metal and the pineapple became known in the colonies as the "hospitality fruit."

During the past four hundred years, through careful selection and cultivation, the pineapple's seeds have been eliminated and its taste has been improved markedly. It is now juicier, sweeter, and much larger than the native fruit grown by the Indians. Strangely enough, no one has been able to develop the wild plants that are still found in Brazil and the West Indies into the delicious fruit Columbus found already under cultivation. This makes us respect the skill of pre-Columbian Indian farmers, who must have experimented for thousands of years to produce the juicy fruit Europeans found under cultivation in the Indies.

Fresh native pineapples, eaten where they are grown, are a pleasant surprise to anyone who has only eaten imported fruit. Pineapples sold on the mainland of the United States are picked green in Hawaii, the Azores, or the West Indies so they won't spoil in shipping. It is a never-to-be-forgotten experience to taste fresh pineapple out of the field where it has ripened under the tropical sun.

Brazil, Mexico, the Philippines, Cuba, and Formosa are major producers of pineapple. Malaya, South Africa, and Australia also grow the fruit, but Hawaii is the leader. Hawaii produces 45 percent of all the canned pineapple in the world and 75 percent of the juice.

Early efforts by Hawaiians to ship pineapples to fruit-hungry prospectors during the gold rush days in California ended in failure—the fruit spoiled enroute. About thirty years later, in 1882, two Hawaiians tried to can pineapples on a kitchen stove, but the product didn't sell well, and they didn't earn enough to continue the experiment.

About the same time, an English horticulturist planted several acres of the wild Kailua pineapples in Hawaii. These native fruits were sweet but small. He exchanged plants with other growers all over the tropical world in an effort to find a better fruit. In 1886, smooth Cayenne pineapples were shipped to him from Florida. They had come to Florida from the West Indies. They thrived in the soil and climate of Hawaii and soon became a favorite.

In 1898 a group of California farmers sailed to Hawaii to homestead and grow pineapples. A year later a young Harvard graduate, James Dole, settled in Hawaii. Dole worked with the homesteaders and others to improve plants and to can the fruit.

There are today about 75,000 acres of pineapple fields in Hawaii, where the tropical climate is ideal for its growth. Hawaii's well-drained soil, which was once volcanic ash, supports the strong root-stocks that hold the heavy plant erect.

Pineapples do not grow from seeds, and they do not produce fruit until almost two years after the plants are set out. Three parts of the mature plant are used to start new plants—the "slips" that grow out of the stem just below the fruit, the "suckers" that grow out of the main stem, and the "crowns," which are the spines or leaves at the top of the fruit.

These are cut off with sharp, hooked knives and planted in newly prepared fields. Fifteen to twenty thousand plants are set out on each acre. The slips, suckers, and crowns root easily.

When they are about fifteen months old, and two to three feet high, a pink "flowerbud" appears above the leaves in the center of the plant. It is the size and shape of a small pine cone. Tiny purplish-blue flowers bloom at the base of the cone. Each flower stays open one day, and each forms an "eye" which becomes a separate berry-shaped fruit. This expands until the more than a hundred small fruits form a single solid mass. This

single pineapple, growing in the center of each plant, will weigh five to six pounds when it is ready to be picked.

After the first pineapples are picked, the same plants will produce two more crops of good fruits. These will be smaller than the first. Each will be ready to harvest in about one year. The plants are then destroyed and the field will be prepared for a new crop.

Pineapple fields must be irrigated if the rainfall is less than twenty-five inches each year.

A number of insects and pests attack pineapples. Particularly destructive are mealy bugs, which have in the past nearly destroyed the entire crop in Hawaii. The mealy bug is a tiny, fuzzy-white insect that is found all over the world. It is a sucking pest that has no means of moving about. Ants transport the bug, carrying it in their mouths from plant to plant. The ant draws the sweet pineapple juice from the bug's body without harming it. Busy ants can turn a field of pineapples white with mealy bugs and so much juice is sucked from the plants that they soon wilt and die. The ants then carry the mealy bugs to a new field.

Pineapples are harvested by workers who cut off the fruit with sharp, hooked knives, and at the same time break off the crown of spines on the top. The fruit is then sorted into bins according to size. In commercial growing in Hawaii the fruit is cleaned with a water spray as it moves on a conveyor belt to a machine called a "ginaca." In a rapid series of operations, the ginaca removes the shell, cuts off both ends of the pineapple, and punches out the core. Each fruit is then a cylinder of gold. The ginaca scrapes the shell for pulp and juice and discards the outer husk, which is almost dry. This discard is later ground into bran and fed to cattle on Hawaiian ranches.

The golden cylinders of pineapple are trimmed at the rate of fifty to a hundred a minute. "Eyes" or bits of shell are trimmed off by hand, and the pineapple cylinders are sprayed with cold water. Then they are sliced or crushed and packed. Millions of gallons of juice are processed in a similar manner.

Few home gardeners attempt to grow pineapple as the Indians once did. The fruit takes too long to mature and its care is too complicated for most home gardeners, even if they live in a tropical climate. Yet anyone can grow a decorative pineapple plant on a windowsill in the house. First, cut off the crown of a pineapple that has been purchased to eat and set it in a shallow dish of water. The crown will grow new spines that resemble cactus spines. The plant may not be edible, but it makes an attractive living decoration, a sign of hospitality, or a symbol of friendship.

❧ 7 ❧

CHOCOLATE AND COCOA

It started with Montezuma—and he had no idea what he was starting. In 1519, the legendary emperor of the Aztecs served chocolate and cocoa to Hernando Cortés and his lieutenants. Montezuma couldn't foresee his fate, nor could he predict that the brown liquid would become the third most important drink in the world, overshadowed only by coffee and tea.

Twenty-five years earlier, Columbus returned to Spain from one of his voyages to the West Indies with seeds or beans from the cacao tree. Columbus told of this strange tree that had large branches that seemed to burst open with patches of small pink flowers. These stemless flowers, which popped out of the bark, grew into melon-shaped pods that clung to the trunk. Cacao pods were green, red, yellow, or purple, depending on their age. The brown seeds in the ripened pods were used as the basis for the drink Montezuma served to his Spanish visitors.

Spain took little notice of the brown seed-beans Columbus carried home from America; the people were too overwhelmed by the other food treasures he had "discovered"—maize, beans, squash, and peanuts. The Spaniards were slow to recognize the immense value of the cacao bean, which is now said to be the most valuable tree crop in the world. It may not have started

with Montezuma, but the Spaniards first appreciated cocoa shortly after Montezuma entertained Cortés in the Aztec chief's elaborate chambers. The emperor offered two native drinks, both well-known to the poorest Aztec but new to the white men.

The unsweetened drink, *cacaoquahitl*, made by boiling roasted cacao beans in water, was a favorite of Montezuma. He drank as many as fifty cups a day. The Spaniards didn't like it until they learned it refreshed them when they were tired. This was vital in the hot, humid climate of Montezuma's world.

A second drink—thick sweet *chocolatl*—was also made from the cacao bean. The Spaniards preferred it to *cacaoquhitl*. Like Montezuma, they sipped it or ate it with long-handled spoons made of gold or tortoise shell.

Before long, the Spaniards had learned the secrets of preparing each drink. They soon mastered the intricate process of preparing the beans and they collected vast quantities of cacao beans for shipment to Spain. For almost a hundred years Spain controlled the cocoa supply from America. Spain jealously guarded the manufacturing secrets Cortés had learned from the Indians. But no one can keep a secret forever. By the early 1600s, French and Italian royal families were buying cacao beans from clever spice traders who somehow managed to get them. Royal chefs made a disappointing bitter cocoa drink—but none of them discovered the secret recipes the Spanish stole from the Indians.

The drink didn't become popular in Europe until Princess Maria Teresa of Spain married Louis XIV of France. Maria Teresa was a cocoa drinker. She gave to France the Aztec's secret recipe to which Spanish chefs had added sugar, spices from the islands of the South Pacific, and vanilla from a long, thin vanilla bean which the Indians had also given the Spanish. Maria Ter-

esa, as Queen of France, served chocolate at many social occasions. The secret was out. It soon leaked from the palace chefs to the many good cooks in France. "Chocolate Houses" sprang up in France, Austria, and Italy, but the price was so high that few but aristocrats could afford the drink.

By 1660, Chocolate Houses were popular in England, and the supply had increased to a point where the general public could now afford to drink cocoa.

The cocoa bean probably originated in the wilds of Peru, Brazil, or the Guianas centuries before Columbus stepped ashore in the New World. Spanish explorers learned only that a tree produced a bean that the Indians called *cacahuatl*. The beans grew inside large pods. When the pods were ripe, Indians cut them off the tree trunks and split them open with a machete. Women and children dug the beans out of the pods. The beans were piled on mats and covered with leaves to make them ferment. The fermentation period lasted from three to ten days, depending on the species of cacao tree.

The Spanish explorers found the fermentation step the most difficult to master. The Indians watched the beans carefully, judging exactly when they were dry enough to produce the best taste. The fermentation period is as necessary today as it was thousands of years ago, and is the key to good flavor in chocolate and cocoa.

When the beans were properly dry, the Indians boiled them in water to produce the unsweetened, bitter drink the Spaniards at first rejected. To make the thicker, concentrated drink the Indians roasted cacao beans slowly over an open fire, then ground them with mortars and stone and removed the hulls. Then, from the powder, they produced a thick paste-like drink, which they sweetened with honey and flavored with vanilla and spices.

This method of preparing the drink is still used by many

back-country families in Central and South America. This drink
may contain a sprinkling of hulls and grit, but it is much the
same as the cocoa that was served in Spain, France, Italy, and
England three hundred years ago.

Cacao trees not only grew wild but were cultivated by the
Aztecs, Mayans, and Incas. No one knows how long they had
been growing the trees. Cups found in Incan graves that are
three or four thousand years old bear designs of cacao pods,
which indicates that Indians were using cocoa that long ago.
There is no doubt they taught the Spaniards both how to prepare a drink from the beans and how to cultivate the trees on
which the beans grew.

The Indians knew that young cacao trees had to have shade
and had to be protected from high winds, so they planted
faster-growing trees among seedling cacaos. These "nurse" trees
—banana, mango, and rubber—were harvested and cut down as
soon as the cacaos grew thick enough to protect each other.

The vast acreage of cacaos that was planted by the Indians
was the sole source of supply for centuries after the time of Columbus and Cortés. For many years that supply was adequate,
although more and more people drank cocoa each year. The
consumption increased when Spaniards learned to add cane
sugar for sweetening and cinnamon from the East Indies to vanilla flavoring from Mexico. The demand for cacao beans increased with the popularity of the chocolate drink. It soared
when a Swiss, M. D. Peters, developed, in 1876, a method for
making milk chocolate.

For the first time, chocolate was eaten in solid form. People
craved milk chocolate and its manufacture revolutionized the
cacao industry. More and more trees were cultivated.

During the next fifty years, equatorial Africa gradually became the largest producer of cacao beans. By 1925, Ghana, Ni-

geria, and Africa's Ivory Coast were supplying two-thirds of the world's cacao bean crop. Production has remained stable, and Africa still produces about two billion pounds of the cacao beans each year.

Most of the world's cacao beans are grown on two- to three-acre plantings owned by small farmers whose families can do all the work. Larger cooperative plantations produce about 10 percent of the world's supply.

In addition to Africa, production remains high in the tropical areas of South America. Venezuela, Ecuador, and Brazil are the chief growers in this area of the cacao tree. These countries, along with the tropical islands of the West Indies, produce about four hundred million pounds annually. Some South Pacific Islands have also successfully cultivated this highly prized tree.

The world's production of cacao trees has not increased since 1950; and there is some evidence the supply is decreasing. Trees have become diseased and have ceased to produce. This concerns both producers of chocolate and the people who eat and drink it.

Many cacao trees are overage—that is, they have been bearing beans for more than twenty-five years. New plantings are not keeping pace with the loss of mature trees. Labor problems and political unrest in the cacao belt of equatorial Africa and South America have hindered both the planting of new trees and the harvesting of ripened pods.

A mature cacao tree produces from twenty to forty bean pods annually. When these beans are dried and ready to ship, the yield from each tree is one to two pounds, including the hulls. An acre of mature trees produces up to three hundred and fifty pounds each year, but only half of this can be used for chocolate or cocoa, the rest is hulls and other waste.

There are many species of the cacao tree. Each bears beans that have a different quality and flavor. Ninety percent of all the beans are of average or medium flavor. Only 10 percent of the trees bear high-quality fruit. The demand for the better beans is great.

The United States purchases about 30 percent of all the cacao beans produced in the world. Chocolate and cocoa processors compete aggressively to obtain a larger share of the better-flavored beans. The best beans are blended with lesser-quality beans with extreme care, much as coffee beans are blended in an attempt to produce the best possible coffee. Chocolate-producing companies jealously guard their blending formulas.

Blending, then roasting, are the first manufacturing steps. The beans are then broken into "nibs" and the hulls are removed. The nibs are then milled, pressing out the butter, which forms a thick, dark liquid called "liquor."

About half the butter is removed from the liquor if cocoa is being made. The de-fatted liquor is then pulverized into powder. The remaining cocoa butter is used to produce semisweet and milk chocolate. For this, milk and granulated sugar are blended into the chocolate liquor. The final processing and refining begins when rolling and kneading machines are fed enough cocoa butter to produce a paste-like mixture. When the chocolate mixture is ready, it is placed in moulds. Before it cools it is formed into the different chocolate products which are packaged for sale. For all our modern techniques, the steps taken to produce Montezuma's chocolate were very much the same.

♫ 8 ♫

SEAFOODS: OYSTERS, SHRIMP, LOBSTER, FISH

"Look! A pearl the size of a thick hazelnut!" a soldier cried to his captain when Hernando de Soto's army was marching through Florida in 1541. "I found it in an oyster."

The Spaniards had seen many pearls in Indian villages. One native woman, in what is now South Carolina, wore long strands of heavy pearls around her neck. When questioned, she permitted the soldiers to enter the burial mounds of her people. There they found large woven baskets filled with pearls. Some were seed pearls, others were the size of peas, and many were as big as hazelnuts. It was the custom of the Indians to bring to their temples every pearl they found in the oysters they gathered to eat. The Spanish realized the Indians knew where great beds of oysters could be found.

This information comes from an account by Garcilaso de la Vega, recently translated into English. His eyewitness record covers de Soto's journey of more than four hundred years ago, when the Floridas included a much larger area than the state of Florida does today. He described how the Indians around the Gulf of Mexico and along the rivers of the south searched for oysters. They used great canoes that were made from hollowed tree trunks. Some larger canoes carried twenty-five or thirty Indians who chanted in rhythm to the stroke of their paddles.

While the oystermen were out, often overnight, the Indians in the village built fires, then let them die down to red coals. When the canoes returned, baskets of oysters were spread on the fire to roast. They tasted good, but many pearls were damaged by smoke and heat. The Spaniards thought it was foolish to spoil all the pearls in cooking fires.

The Indians readily showed the Spanish soldiers the oyster beds along the banks of the rivers that ran into the sea and along the edges of the bays. Oysters thrived in fresh water that was mixed with tidal salt water.

Indian men and women collected oysters in shallow water, using hooked spears or long-handled rakes. In deeper waters, they dived to the mollusk beds and brought up oysters and mussels in their hands.

The Indians also dipped for shrimp. The Indians who lived along the coast of the Gulf of Mexico ate many oysters, fish, and shrimp.

While shrimp was not new to Europeans, the kinds taken from the Gulf were different from those eaten at home. Today, the shrimp industry of the Gulf is important to the food supply of the United States. Of all the seafoods known to the Indians, shrimp now has the greatest dollar value.

A swimming shrimp looks like a small fish with a thin shining

shell and two little knob-eyes that stand out from the head on short stalks. This unusual shellfish is called a crustacean because it wears its skeleton on the outside like a suit of armor. Every few months its body grows too large for its flexible translucent shell and it sheds it and forms a larger covering. The shrimp does this several times until it is full-grown at about ten months, when it is ready to eat.

The demand for shrimp is so great that marine scientists and shrimp fishermen are always searching for new shrimp grounds.

In the United States, the three kinds of shrimp most in demand are the large white, the brown, and the pink species. Each of these is native to the Gulf of Mexico, whose warm water has been the world's greatest shrimp "factory" for a little more than thirty years.

For many years Americans could buy only the smaller shallow-water shrimp found along the Atlantic shore from North Carolina to the Gulf Coast of Florida. Then, in 1938, fishermen discovered new shrimp beds off the Mississippi River Delta of Louisiana. There, in the warm salt water of the Gulf, draggers found white shrimp with tails six to seven inches long—the "jumbos." People liked the large white shrimp, but fishermen couldn't keep up with the demand for them and they couldn't find new beds of jumbos.

One day in 1940 a shrimp boat out of Port Isabel, Texas, returned with a new kind of shrimp. They were as large as the jumbos, but brownish in color, which made them difficult to sell. Buyers thought they were beginning to spoil. The fishermen solved this by calling them "Golden Brazilian Shrimp." The demand soon brought an urgent search for new beds.

Soon fishermen discovered another very large species of shrimp in the Gulf. These were called "red shrimp" because of their dark, wine color. This foot-long shrimp is difficult to drag for, since it lives at a depth of 1,000 to 2,000 feet below the surface. Fishermen are experimenting for ways to net it, and the day may soon come when the big wine-colored shrimp will be taken in deep water and marketed profitably.

At present, far more large pink shrimp are marketed than any other kind. Several hundred million pounds are netted each year in the Dry Tortugas off the Florida coast and in the Bay of Campeche, Mexico.

The discovery of the pink shrimp beds hung upon the difference between day and night. In the late 1940s shrimpers sometimes found a few of a new kind of shrimp in their nets in the Florida Keys and fishermen were surprised to find the new large pink shrimp in the stomachs of fish.

Two brothers, veteran shrimpers in St. Augustine, Florida, heard stories about the new shrimp. They went to the Keys, rented an old fishing boat and dragged the trawl or nets on the bottom from the Florida Keys to the Dry Tortugas, searching from sunup to sundown, as they had caught shrimp off St. Augustine.

After two days of hauling in nets filled with crabs, starfish, sponges, and small fish, but no shrimp, they decided their search was a failure. Yet they knew this new shrimp lived somewhere.

It was growing dark, but they decided to make one final run with the trawl. When it was hauled up, the lights on the boat were reflected from the glowing knob-eyes of thousands of large pink shrimp! The shrimpers shouted as if they had found gold. They realized why these shrimp hadn't been found earlier. Unlike white shrimp, which men had always netted in daylight, the large pink species fed at *night* and buried themselves in the mud by day and the shrimper's nets hadn't disturbed their siesta.

The discoverers tried to keep their find a secret, but before long others came and Key West soon became a famous shrimp port. Today, more than twenty years later, Key West is one of the chief shrimp ports of the world.

As shrimp became more important as a food, the United States Bureau of Marine Fisheries and the Fish and Wildlife Service intensified their study of the life cycle of shrimp, and scientists of the Institute of Marine Science at the University of Miami, Florida, with private funds carefully studied the life phases of the pink shrimp.

Scientists had long suspected there was a direct relationship between the very small young shrimp that were found in the brackish sawgrass areas of the Florida Everglades and the large adult shrimp that were being harvested a hundred miles away near the Dry Tortugas. To prove this theory, they strung nets in the estuaries of the Everglades and caught baby shrimp, which they injected with dye. The juvenile shrimp were then released in the same waters. Some months later, shrimp boats far out in the Gulf netted dye-marked shrimp. This proved that young shrimp that grew up in the shallow waters of the Everglades migrated a hundred miles out into the Gulf. Knowing this, the scientists wondered where the adult shrimp laid their eggs and where the eggs hatched.

Scientists then studied female shrimp that had been netted near the Dry Tortugas and found they were ready to lay eggs. Young shrimp must hatch a hundred miles or more out at sea!

A female shrimp lays between three hundred thousand to a million eggs. These hatch in a few hours to larvae, which can scarcely be seen without a magnifying glass. The larvae are nourished for about thirty-six hours by the yolk of the egg—then the dot-sized shrimp must find food or die.

If they remain in deep water they may be eaten by fish or bigger shrimp, but there is safety in the quiet waters of the Everglades. It seemed impossible that such minute creatures could swim a hundred miles, yet test-netting at intervals from the spawning grounds to the shallow Everglades estuaries revealed that not only did the tiny shrimp travel this incredible distance, but they did so in ten days' time! The most probable theory is that they ride the incoming flood tide toward the Everglades. When the tide ebbs, they cling to the sandy sea bottom, then emerge for another ride on the next flood tide.

Studies by marine biologists and conservationists also revealed that young shrimp remained in the Everglades area for ten or eleven months. When they were three to four inches long they left their quiet home to mate and spawn in the Dry Tortugas bed where they had been hatched almost a year before.

We now realize that the Everglades National Park waters are both a massive marine nursery and an invaluable wildlife refuge.

Before the brown and the pink species were discovered, all shrimp netted in the Gulf of Mexico were the white day-feeders. Now less than 10 percent of all shrimp catches are white, which means that 90 percent of shrimp dragging is done at night.

Shrimpers are hardy men, accustomed to riding out sudden tropical storms. Night trawling added new hazards, for it was more difficult for two boats to work together, each dragging one end of the trawl. Collisions and chaos made it necessary to develop new methods for handling the trawls.

Modern shrimp boats drag "otter-board" trawls—nets about sixty to a hundred feet long with large floats on the upper lip. The otter-board consists of two boards that are about ten feet long and as wide as the door of a house. One board is attached at each end of the net. These boards keep the mouth of the net open so it will sweep a wide area of the bottom. Using otter-boards, each boat is an independent unit, a much safer way to trawl.

A boat does not fill its hold with shrimp in one night. Usually the trawl is dragged for several hours. If it collects a few hundred pounds of shrimp, the trawl is considered a success.

The haul is dumped on the deck and there are invariably all sorts of sea creatures mixed with the shrimp.

As soon as the trawl is lowered to drag again, the crew sorts the "trash" creatures from the shrimp, shoveling the rejects overboard. The shrimpers remove the shrimp's heads by hand, breaking off and saving only the tails. These are washed, then iced or placed in chilled sea water in the hold. After about a week of this night work, the boat returns to port to unload its catch and take on supplies of water and food for the next trip.

At the dock the shrimp are washed again in tanks of salt water before they are iced and packed in crates for immediate shipment in refrigerator trucks.

Shrimping is an important industry and marine scientists are trying to find new methods to increase the natural production of shrimp. They are also searching for ways to produce shrimp by "marine farming."

"Farming" shrimp has strong possibilities but attempts so far have been disappointing. Experiments are being conducted in widely scattered areas of the United States to determine whether bare estuaries can be seeded with live juvenile shrimp from natural shrimp nurseries such as the Everglades. If these experiments even prove successful in only a fraction of the new areas, the shrimp industry will be strengthened. Similar experiments are being made in other parts of North and South America, Europe, and Asia.

A second—successful—method of shrimp farming is now being practiced in Japan, but the price of these homegrown shrimp range from three to four dollars a pound, higher than the price of shrimp netted at sea.

A related method of "farming" is to net small wild shrimp in their natural grounds and place the juveniles in pens until they reach maturity. This method is fairly common in Indonesia,

India, Japan, and the Philippines. The major problem in all types of shrimp farming is to supply enough natural food to keep the young shrimp from dying of starvation or from eating each other. These problems may some day be overcome, but until then we must depend on men at sea with a boat and trawl.

Lobsters are another natural food that still are only taken from the sea. Many Indian tribes along the shores of New England knew how to *trap* lobsters long before they showed the Pilgrims how to *eat* them. Long-buried shell heaps have been found from Maine to south of Cape Cod. Many tribes summered in New England, where they enjoyed huge feasts of lobsters, oysters, steamer clams, and quahogs. Bits of pottery and other artifacts that can be traced to tribes as far west as Wisconsin and Minnesota have been found in the "digs" or mounds of buried shells along our eastern shores.

William Bradford's journal of the life at Plymouth describes Indians showing Pilgrims how to tramp the mud banks along creeks to find eels to eat, and how to dig for soft shell clams. Later the Indians taught the settlers how to trap—and eat—lobster.

Lobsters are still taken individually from the sea in traps or "pots." Lobstermen can't "drag" for lobster as shrimpers trawl for shrimp. Lobstering is often lonely work where one or two men will own and set their pots.

Almost daily in summer each lobsterman goes out in his small boat and hauls up his pots by hand or by means of a mechanized winch. He takes out any lobster that may be trapped there, then rebaits and lowers the pot. A lobsterman may have only enough pots to supply his own family, or he may have hundreds if he sells commercially. He can never be sure he will find a catch, which is one reason that lobster is often in short supply and high-priced.

Another reason is that lobsters take a long time to grow to eating size. When a lobster is born, it is doubled into a ball about the size of a pea and drifts on the surface of the water. While it is growing it may be tossed ashore by storms, killed by man-made pollution such as oil spills, or eaten by fish.

It feeds on plankton and other minute organisms which float in the water. Lobsters will often eat each other. They also can grow a new claw if they lose one. A lobster grows about one inch longer each year. Every two years it molts, its hard shell breaking from the larger shell forming underneath. Until the new soft shell hardens, it hides on the bottom of the sea under rocks. It takes about eight years for a lobster to reach eating size, or one and a quarter pounds. Some older lobsters grow much larger and weigh ten pounds or more when caught.

Fishing was important to any tribe that lived near the seas, along rivers, or on lakes. Each tribe had its own way of making weirs or fish traps from tree boughs, cane, or reed. On the Pacific Coast, Indians trapped and speared migrating salmon. In spring Indians along the Great Lakes caught sturgeon as they left the lakes for the rivers. Indians often shot the larger fish with bows and arrows.

In winter Indians taught settlers how to cut fishing holes in the ice on frozen lakes. Then they waited, spear in hand, luring fish to the hole by dipping a bright feather or a scrap of cloth up and down.

In summer tribesmen often speared the fish at night from a canoe with a lighted bark torch at the bow. One Indian sat in the stern and paddled while another in the bow speared any curious fish that was lured too close by the light.

Indians ate fresh fish that was baked over coals, or in fish stews—much as campers do today. They also dried fish and smoked them for the long cold winters.

Seafoods were known to Europeans long before they reached the New World, yet a knowledge of *where* to find certain seafoods in an unfamiliar environment, and *how* best to use the catch was a direct and open gift from native Indians to the early settlers.

⧓ 9 ⧓

INDIAN MAIZE, OR CORN

1: *Its Mysterious Origin*

Corn is the most important food the Indians have given us. The source of corn—or maize—is also the most mysterious of any of the Indian foods. No one has ever found maize growing wild and scientists have never found a wild grass plant that even resembles corn.

There is a *teocentli* grass in Mexico that may be distantly related to corn, but botanists have not been able to produce a corn plant from it.

There must have been a kind of corn plant growing wild in areas that are now known as Mexico, New Mexico, and Arizona when the first people reached that part of America between twenty-five and fifty thousand years ago. Drill core samples from two hundred feet below the surface of the earth in Mexico City prove this.

To get a core sample, scientists drive a hollow pipe deep into the earth. When the pipe is pulled up, scientists study the core of soil to learn about the ancient people, plants, and artifacts that have been covered by thousands of years of dust and debris.

Carbon-14 tests on drill core samples in Mexico City revealed corn pollen that was eighty thousand years old! This was long before the first Asiatic hunters arrived on the American continents. These roaming tribes probably came by way of a thirty-six-mile land bridge that joined Asia and Alaska before it sank into the Bering Sea. This was also many years before these nomadic hunters became farmers who grew food plants and settled in villages.

Long ago the wild corn died, but before it did, men had started to cultivate the plant. Over many years Indians developed corn with larger and larger ears. Scientists have found tiny ears of corn in digs inside dry caves in New Mexico, Arizona, and Mexico. This corn is at least seven thousand years old. In some New Mexican caves they found ears of corn that were the size of large strawberries, and still deeper they found older ears that were as small as a penny.

Such digs prove that Indians cultivated wild corn for thousands of years in many parts of America and that they gradually improved the plants until corn became an important source of dependable food. Great Indian empires were founded on corn.

Without maize there could never have been an Aztec civilization in Mexico, a Mayan civilization in Central America, or the fabulous Empire of the Incas in South America. People must have a secure food supply before they can build a civilization, and corn was just such a food supply. Corn gave Indians the

freedom to paint, weave cloth, design pottery, engrave bone or shells, and fashion beautiful objects in silver or gold.

By the time Columbus found the New World, Indians had been improving corn for at least six thousand years. Maize had spread from its probable source in Mexico to most parts of North and South America.

The earliest white explorers described maize in their reports of voyages to America. Norsemen who visited the northeast coast of North America in the eleventh century reported that the *skraellings,* as the Vikings called the Indians, sowed fields of maize.

In November 1492, Columbus sent two seamen to explore the island that was later named Cuba. They returned to the ship with the report that the natives grew "a grain they call maize, which is well tasted, bak'd, dryed, and made into flour."

Records of de Soto's journey of discovery through the southeastern part of the United States in 1541–1542 state that every tribe grew corn, "a grass which means the same to all the Indians of the New World as wheat does to Spain."

In Mississippi the Chickasaw Indians gave the Spaniards "corn and dried fruit, and mats of woven corn husks to keep them warm." In Arkansas, Spaniards spent six months of winter with the Indians and "gathered corn, though it is a fact that already there was as much of it in the town as to be practically enough for the entire season."

John Smith wrote that the settlers of Jamestown, Virginia, in 1607 would have starved if the Indians had not brought corn, squash, and beans to them.

Governor William Bradford wrote in his history of Plymouth that the Pilgrims found baskets of corn buried by the Indians on Cape Cod. This corn proved to be the difference between life and death, for the Pilgrims used the seed for their first planting the next spring. Bradford records they later gave gifts to the Pamet Indians in payment for the corn.

Corn soon became the most important food in pioneer America. Colonists even paid their rent, taxes, and debts with corn, for there was very little "hard money." Governor Bradford reported sending bushels of maize back to England to repay the "Adventurers," those men who had loaned the Pilgrims money to buy supplies for their voyage to the New World.

The Indians of North and South America recognized how important corn was to them. The word maize means both "bread-of-life" and "grain-of-the-Gods." The Indians also knew that corn did not grow wild and was different from any other plant. With no knowledge of how corn had come down to them over thousands of years, they believed corn was a direct gift of the gods.

Each tribe had its own legend of how corn came to man, and each was the story of a miracle. Typical was the Iroquois legend, which held that in a time of great famine a spirit woman walked the earth with pity. In the prints of her moccasins, corn sprang up to feed the people.

Most tribes honored maize in annual religious ceremonies or festivals of thanksgiving. Tribesmen often wore corn-husk masks while they danced, waving green stalks above their heads and singing corn's praises.

The Incas of Peru held the most elaborate ceremonies. They believed maize was a sacred gift from their Sun God, Inti. The nobility drank a corn drink, *chicha*, from cups of gold that were fashioned in the shape of ears of corn. In their temple gardens, Incas set up stalks of corn. The kernels were gold and the husks and silks were silver. The common Indian farmers of Peru buried small clay or wooden "charms" in their fields to encourage the corn to grow.

French colonists who came into the lower Mississippi valley in the late 1500s found that the Natchez Indians called their chief the Great Sun and worshiped corn in much the same way as the sun worshipers of South America.

The Iroquois and related tribes in northeastern United States planted corn, beans, and squash in the same fields, saying that the three "sister spirits" wished to live together.

Along the Gulf Coast and through Georgia, Arkansas, North Carolina, and Tennessee, the Spanish found Indians living in villages that were built around a central square that was carefully brushed for ceremonies. Their green corn holiday, *puskita,* was a time of the renewal of life. Old fires were put out, worn pottery was broken, and the village was cleaned. Each tribesman was supposed to forget and forgive all old quarrels and begin anew.

It is exciting to compare this Indian green corn ceremony with a spring ceremony of the Celts of Wales, Scotland, and Ireland, who also put out old fires and ended old quarrels to begin each growing season. The more historians, scientists, and archaeologists study Indians, the more they realize how much there is to learn about their origins.

Indians of the many tribes are so different in appearance, customs, and languages that historians believe they had different origins. Perhaps small groups of men from other civilizations reached the Americas by boat long before Columbus. Unable to return to their homelands, they mixed with the descendants of the earlier Asiatic tribes that had crossed the Bering Strait.

Professor von Wuthenau of the University of Aujuicas in Mexico City stated recently that a Mayan figure had been found wearing a Star of David earring. Professor Gordon of Brandeis University reported that a stone found in a burial mound in Tennessee shows a design in the style of the Israelites. The professors believe that Mediterranean Jews, refugees from the Roman wars, may have reached America as early as A.D. 700.

Professor von Wuthenau also believes that before A.D. 300, a few Egyptians, Chinese, Japanese, and possibly African blacks may have crossed the oceans to the Americas. In the New World they mingled their skills and languages with those of the earlier Indians. A Brazilian archaeologist claims he has found evidence of a Phoenician civilization in South America. These Old World people, he states, used copper and lead in the New World thousands of years before the Incas made beautiful figurines from gold, silver, and copper.

The history of the Indians is still largely a mystery, as is the origin of corn. The two puzzles are related and may be solved together, since new knowledge is gained each year through archaeological digs and chance discoveries.

For example, in 1927 near Folsom, New Mexico, for the first time in the United States men found a spearpoint embedded in the ribs of a prehistoric bison, proving that man lived in the Americas during the Ice Age, before that particular bison disappeared. It was not until 1948 that archaeologists found the tiny cobs of corn in Bat Cave in New Mexico and La Perra Cave in Mexico. Only recently bones and artifacts of ancient Indians were found behind the home of a farm family on a small island in a river in Illinois. Scientists from Northwestern University have made a twenty-nine-foot dig and have found skeletons and corn which carbon-tested to be about 4,500 years old. They believe there is an older layer of artifacts below, at a depth of thirty-four feet, but it is under the watertable and cannot be excavated until funds are provided to continue the work. Careful excavation work is expensive.

In late 1971 skin divers in Mineral Springs in south Florida found underwater ledges with skeletons of men, ancient mastodons, giant land turtles, and a sloth, all of which have been extinct for a very long time. They were wonderfully preserved by salt water at depths of twenty, forty, and ninety feet.

A few miles away, in an old, deep sink hole that was hidden

by palms and brush, divers found tools, leaves, and acorns and the skeletons of men and animals. These had also been preserved by salt waters for fifty centuries!

Archaeologists pounce on each new find, eager to learn more about the origins and lives of ancient Indians. Whether they will discover anything new about corn remains to be seen, but one thing is certain—much is still to be learned.

2: *What* Is *Known About Corn*

Corn spread mile by mile, century by century, north, east, south, and west until it ruled as the king of foods among the tribes in both North and South America. Of the many food crops developed by Indian farmers, corn spread over the greatest area and had the greatest impact.

Only twenty-five years after Columbus carried seed kernels back to Spain, introducing it to the Old World, corn had spread across Europe, and within fifty years maize was being grown throughout most of the world. Today it ranks second only to wheat as a staple world food crop, and it is well ahead of the next two most important food plants—rice and potatoes.

Modern corn varies greatly in the size of the stalk and the ears. It ranges from two-inch ears of pod corn that is grown high in the Andes Mountains of South America to fabulous three-foot ears that are produced in Mexico's Jala Valley. The stalks of this Mexican corn are so strong they are used for fence posts!

Sometime during the long period when maize was being developed and the wild plant disappeared, corn lost its natural heartiness and became as helpless as a newborn babe. Indian farmers had given their fields of corn tender loving care and the plant was no longer able to survive without man's help. Corn does not re-seed itself well, and weeds will kill the young plants. Today's corn could disappear from the earth in a short time if man didn't cultivate it.

Corn needed so much care and was so important to Indians that tribes rarely went to war during the planting and cultivating seasons. When the harvest came, they pulled the ears from the stalks and hid their precious corn in caches for winter. They buried it underground in baskets that were covered with deerskin and sealed with pitch tar, or it was stored in earthen mounds above ground. In the colder climates it was sometimes sewed inside dried animal skins and hung high in trees.

Through the ages Indian farmers developed most of our "modern" methods of growing corn. The first step was to select the very best ears for seed corn. They soon learned to plant especially good strains in separate fields. This is still done today to produce "pure" varieties of corn.

Three to four thousand years ago Indian farmers learned to cross carefully the pollen of two or more pure strains. Today this cross-pollination is called hybridizing. By the time Columbus arrived in the New World, Indians were growing corn in a variety of sizes and colors. Some ears had kernels as small as beads, while the kernels of others were as large as a twenty-five-cent piece. There were yellow, red, white, blue, chocolate brown, gray, and black ears. Some ears were a mixture of several colors.

The Indians had also developed varieties of maize that grew at high altitudes, fourteen thousand feet up in the Andes Mountains. Very different kinds grew at sea level.

Pre-Incan farmers get most of the credit for developing corn, for their engineers had built irrigation systems that were as great as any the world has ever seen. Some of these are still

carrying water after thousands of years of use. These Indians also understood the use of fertilizers. The Incas used *guano*— bird droppings—that they brought by canoe from coastal islands where great flocks of birds congregated. Using *guano*, they cultivated crop after crop of corn on the same fields year after year. The Mayas, who used very little fertilizer, had learned to "rest" their fields to restore fertility. They grew corn on the same land only once every four to seven years. In Mexico, the Aztecs also changed their growing fields each year, unless they could collect bat droppings in nearby caves.

Indians in Florida used the widespread deposits of phosphates for fertilizer, and Indians along the northeastern Atlantic coast used fish, as did many tribes along inland rivers and lakes.

Whatever the method, and wherever they were, Indian farmers developed six different kinds of corn—dent, sweet, pod, flint, flour, and popcorn. No new type of corn has been produced by modern man, although the various strains have been improved in quality and quantity.

For four hundred years each new wave of European settlers in the United States planted corn much as the Indians had and they produced about the same yield to the acre. Only during the last fifty years or so have farmers made significant changes in corn production. Improved cultivation, fertilization, weed and insect control, and the new hybrid corn seed have helped American farmers raise the per-acre yield three-fold.

The pointed digging stick and primitive hoe used by Indians are long gone, and no one would dream of using a sharpened piece of bone, fastened to his hand, to slash an ear of corn from the stalk and the husks from the ear. Even the steel husking hook that was used by American settlers is a relic of the past, and the hand-guided plow, which was pulled by oxen or horses or a sturdy farm wife, have all but disappeared. They have been replaced with heavy machinery that plows, plants, cultivates, and harvests some fifty million acres of corn in the United States each year.

This country's Corn Belt is one hundred fifty million acres of the richest farmland in the world. It is an area so large that it takes several days to cross it by car—either east and west, north and south. Nine Corn Belt states—Illinois, Iowa, Indiana, Minnesota, Nebraska, Missouri, Ohio, Wisconsin, and South Dakota —produce the greatest share of the nation's annual harvest of five billion bushels.

Such a figure staggers the imagination. It is especially impressive when you consider that the world's annual corn harvest is eleven billion bushels.

As early as 1933 the United States Congress passed laws that limited the number of acres that could be planted in corn. These laws were designed to support the price, for it was believed that low prices would discourage farmers from planting corn. The laws were enforced, but creative farmers, aided by state and university experimental stations, were soon producing twice as much corn on much less acreage. Since the 1930s the Congress has added more controls. The cultivated corn acreage has dropped from seventy-six million to fifty-five million, yet the average yield has risen in the same period from thirty-seven to eighty-five bushels per acre.

Improved hybrid seed is responsible for much of the increased harvest. Some farmers make a business of isolating and growing pure strains of corn, which are crossed to produce high-yield hybrid seed. Today most farmers buy seed from the hybrid growers. Hybrid seed is more expensive than the field corn he grows, but if a farmer consistently used kernels from his own fall harvest his yield per acre would decline. Whether he realizes it or not, pre-Columbian Indians taught him that!

Corn is planted in May in the Corn Belt, and there is an expression that it should be "knee high by the Fourth of July." The corn stalk will begin to sprout ears in fairly early July, followed immediately by the growth of a tassel on top of the plant. This tassel distinguishes corn from all other plants. It is the corn plant's flower, made up of a fountain of fronds with hundreds of tiny blue-pink flowers. Pollen drops from these tassels to fertilize the "silks" that spring from the top of the ears. The silvery silks are long and thread-like. Each grows from a point on the cob inside the green husks. The silks push out of the husks to receive the pollen and each silk strand conducts pollen to the cob and starts the growth of a kernel. By September the kernels are hardening under the green husks and the corn can be harvested through October. A frost in mid-October will help loosen the husks on the ripened ears, but farmers try to complete their husking in November before the first heavy snowfall.

"Dent," or field corn, is the king of maize. It grows mile after green mile across the face of middle America. Dent corn's ears are about a foot long and heavy with 900 to 1000 kernels on each cob. Nine out of ten ears—or nine *million* out of every ten *million* bushels harvested—are fed to live stock or poultry. Corn fattens most of the meat marketed in this country. One ear out of ten is used for many things—from cooking oil to varnish. The following is a partial list of the widespread use of corn:

Food for man:	Food for livestock:	Corn by-products:
baby foods	corn bran	alcohol
canned, frozen sweet corn	corn fodder and silage	antifreeze
candy	cornmeal cake	ceramics
chewing gum	whole kernels	cosmetics
		dyes

cookies
cooking oil
cornflakes
cornmeal
cornstarch
corn sugar
corn syrup
hominy and grits
margarine
salad dressings
vinegar
yeast

ether
explosives
insulating materials
medicines
paints
paper
paperboard
pastes and binders
photographic film
plastics
safety glass
soaps
solvents
textiles
varnishes

Next to dent, sweet corn ranks second in production volume. Sweet corn has smaller, sweeter ears than dent and was developed by Indians for eating in the "milk," or soft-kernel stage. Sweet corn is canned for market or sold fresh in its husks. It tastes best if it is husked immediately after it has been picked, cooked quickly in boiling water, and eaten "on the cob" with butter, pepper, and salt.

Popcorn is known everywhere. Massassoit presented it to the Pilgrims for their first Thanksgiving feast, but long before that the Incas were growing this unique exploding corn. Pottery cornpoppers have been found in excavations in Peru. They are remarkably similar to a modern skillet with a lid.

Today most of the popcorn in the United States is produced in a few counties in Nebraska and Iowa, although it will grow in many states. Popcorn is as easy to grow as sweet corn in a home garden.

Flint corn is the many-colored maize the Indians were growing when the first colonists arrived in Virginia and Massachusetts. It is still grown in some parts of the world for food, but it is tough eating, for its colorful kernels are as hard as flint. Americans decided it is better to look at than it is to eat.

The strangest variety of maize is pod corn. Each pod-corn kernel has its own husk. Pod corn is almost more bother than it is worth and it is only grown by isolated native farmers in a few tropical areas of America.

The earliest Americans learned to remove the tough skins from corn kernels, possibly by accident when some corn spilled into a cooking fire. Later, when rain fell on the cold ashes, lye was formed and this lye peeled the skins from the kernels. One way or another, Indians then learned to soak corn in lyewater to remove the skins. The tender inner kernels were washed and boiled to make hominy or were ground into small granules called grits. Grits are a popular food in the South and flavored hominy appears on millions of breakfast tables as cornflakes.

The most common food used by Indians was a coarse cornmeal that was made by pounding corn between two stones. The flat stone on which the Mayans ground corn was called a *metate*. Indian women spend endless hours removing dry corn kernels from the cobs, then pounding the kernels until the meal was fine. This cornmeal was mixed with water and shaped by hand into flat thin cakes which were baked on clay griddles. American settlers also used corn for cakes—the legendary "Johnnycakes." The plain flat cakes made by Indians were nourishing, portable, and could be eaten without other foods—but they had a distressing lack of flavor. The Indians devised many ways to give them spice or character. Mexican Indians and tribes of the West Indies loved peppers, the hotter the better, so they mixed hot peppers into the wet cornmeal before baking

their cakes. Other Indians dipped the corn cakes into a hot pepper sauce before they ate them.

To make an even tastier cake, Indians mixed beanmeal with cornmeal and peppers. These cakes were called *tamales*. Some Indians rolled the meat from roasted birds—wild turkey or quail —into the tamale cakes. This was one of the Indian foods that the early Spaniards liked best when they sampled the native cuisine.

Today, in Mexico and southwestern United States, tamales are a popular food. The raw dough is rolled around minced, highly seasoned meat and the tamale is often placed in a corn husk before it is steamed over a slow fire.

Another popular Indian food that has survived for thousands of years is the tortilla (*tor-tee-yah*). This is a thin, round cake that is made of cornmeal. It is often as large as a dinner plate. For centuries tortillas have been baked on clay griddles that are carefully heated so the cake won't get too dry and break when it is later rolled into a cylinder or tube. Tortillas are served hot from the griddle. Each diner rolls his or her own tortillas, which are then used as scoops to dip up pepper sauce or other foods.

Some Indians, particularly the Mayas, made a third corn food that is far less well known—a drink called *pozole* (*poh-so-lay*). Isolated Central American tribes still prepare this nourishing drink. To produce it, women first mix a fine powdered cornmeal with water to make a dough. They knead the dough by hand, shaping it into dough-balls that are about the size of a walnut. At their customary two meals a day, morning and evening, the Indians dissolved these dough balls in water and the *pozole* was served in gourds. Men and women at work in the fields carried balls of corn dough and gourds of water for a snack when they rested, and children often drank *pozole* between meals.

Indians of both North and South America looked forward each season to feasts of the first sweet corn or roasting ears. The green ears, with husks still on, were roasted over coals of fire or they were steamed for a short time over hot stones in a fire pit. Usually the pit was covered with animal skins or seaweed to keep in the heat.

North American Indians taught the white settlers, trappers, and hunters to dry sweet corn for winter food. Indians sliced off the milky kernels from the ripened ear, dried the kernels in the hot sun, and stored them for winter or for travel. Sweet corn was watched daily and picked at its best, when the kernels were full and milky. It was tested by pricking sample kernels with a thumbnail. If it didn't spout milk, the corn was too old.

Some people—both Indians and their imitators—dried corn directly from the field. Others blanched it. To blanch corn, green ears were husked and the cobs were dropped into a kettle of boiling water for a minute or two. The ears were then dipped out and cooled.

There is a knack to cutting corn off the cob. The cob should be held upright, on its flat end, one hand holding it by the top. Then, with a sharp knife, cut downward the whole length of the rows. Cut evenly and deep enough to slice off most of the whole kernel, but not deep enough to get any of the cob. The kernels should fall away in milky slabs, moist and sticky. The cobs are then scraped with the knife to remove any corn that remains. Spread the cut kernels on a clean white cloth outdoors in the sunshine and cover the corn with a thinner cloth such as cheese-cloth to protect it from flies and birds. The hot sun will dry the corn in a few days. If rain threatens, the cloth and corn should be carried inside. Sun-dried corn may be stored in cloth bags that are hung in an attic or some other dry place. In winter, then as now, the shriveled kernels are soaked in water to restore them to their original shape and size, then boiled a few minutes. When butter, milk, a pinch of salt, and perhaps a little sugar are added, dried corn can be almost as delicious as fresh corn straight from the field.

It is easy to see that corn influenced, even controlled, the lives of early Indians and the settlers who invaded their lands. Corn was the single most important source of food, although it has always been the most difficult of American food plants to grow. Corn must have ten to twelve inches of rain during its growing season, yet too much rain will destroy it. Weeds are its greatest enemy; if *they* flourish, the young corn dies. Corn prefers a rich soil but it will grow in poorer soils if that soil is fertilized and irrigated.

Canadians grow a variety of corn that matures in sixty to seventy days, which is the normal warm season between the killing frosts in the north. In the Corn Belt of the United States, corn has much longer—about one hundred twenty days—to mature, and in the tropics, more than one crop can be grown in a year.

In the high altitude of the Andes, Indian farmers developed a corn that would continue to grow *after* a freeze.

Corn is adaptable, but it is also susceptible to more diseases and insect damage than any other major food plant. It has so many natural enemies that it requires constant protection in order to survive. Farmers must guard against legions of insects that attack from all sides—at corn's roots, stalk, leaves, and its kernels. Corn is also vulnerable to rot, blight, and a dark fungus called smut. Flocks of crows and other birds attack the ends of the ears while the kernels are in the milk stage—if they allow it to grow at all and don't eat the newly planted seed corn.

Birds also have a taste for the mature kernels after a freeze loosens the husks, and only the tight covering of husks saves it from total destruction by birds, mice, and rats.

A prudent and hard-working farmer can control most of the corn's enemies, but it requires a constant and continuing fight. Progress has been made in developing non-toxic weed and pest controls that won't build up in the soil and in living creatures, but much work remains to be done. Corn is important to the world's well being; the environment is vital.

The Western Hemisphere was built on Indian maize, and we still depend on it for much of our daily food. Corn is more closely tied to its Indian origins than any other known food plant, and we owe a considerable debt to generations of Indian farmers who nursed it down through the years. No one knows where this valuable and mysterious plant started its journey, but it is man's good fortune that its travels have carried it around the world.

❧ 10 ❧

OTHER FOODS THE INDIANS GAVE US

STRAWBERRIES

Roger Williams wrote that he found the Indians of New England growing strawberries. "In some parts, where the natives have planted, I have seen—within a few miles—as many strawberries as would fill a good ship."

He was speaking of a small strawberry that English colonists also found both growing wild and used by Indians in Virginia in 1607. A similar small strawberry also grew in Europe, where it sold for about $30 a pound. The wild Virginia strawberry was later crossed with the European variety producing a delicious berry that was still too small to have much market value.

About this time French agriculturists learned that the Span-

iards had found Indians growing red, white, and yellow strawberries that were as big as pears. They were excited, since
strawberries that large could bring a good price in the market.

Determined to get some of the huge American strawberries,
the French sent a plant expert, disguised as a Spanish seaman,
to South America. His mission: bring back seeds from the giant
strawberries. The Frenchman finally sneaked back to France
with the seeds, but he and his fellow agriculturists were in for a
disappointment—the strawberries were big and beautiful, but
they tasted like wood, not sweet like the smaller European and
wild North American berries. Eager to increase the size of
strawberries, experts cross-pollinated the giant Indian berries
with Virginia and European varieties. The result was a huge
success. The offshoot of the three plants, found so far apart, was
large and red and sweet and juicy. Since then, dozens of varieties have been developed. All are directly related to the berries
found in North and South America and Europe.

About half a billion pounds of strawberries are grown commercially in the United States each year. Strawberries are
grown in each of the fifty states as well as in Canada and Mexico. California produces the most, followed by Oregon, Michigan, Florida, Louisiana, and New Jersey.

Strawberries are eaten fresh, canned, frozen, or as preserves.
They are expensive, for they must be hand-picked and they
spoil quickly. They grow well in home gardens. Twenty-five to
fifty plants, set out in the spring or fall, produce all the strawberries an average family will use. The two general kinds are
June-bearing, with fruit that ripens all at one time; and ever-
bearing, with berries that ripen during the entire season. The
best plants for a given area may be purchased from a nursery
or seed catalog, which will also provide good directions for planting and raising healthy, delicious berries.

PEPPERS—HOT AND COOL OR SWEET

Like potatoes and tomatoes, peppers are a member of the poisonous nightshade family. Hot, cool, or sweet, peppers originated in South and Central America. Engraved pottery from pre-Incan graves prove that ancient Indians cultivated a dozen or more varieties. None had been seen in any other part of the world before Columbus found them growing in West Indian gardens.

The Incas called these plants *aji*, but the Spanish thought the fruits tasted much like the black powder that was ground from small seeds that was grown in the Orient. The Spanish changed the Indian *aji* to *pimientas*, or peppers. Later, people often called peppers by their Aztec name *chili*.

More than thirty kinds of peppers are grown all over the world. Some are merely decorative: they are bright red, yellow, and white. But most peppers, whatever their color, are used for seasoning.

Peppers grow in many shapes and sizes. Some are formed like cones or carrots, while others are shapped like beanpods—wrinkled, flat, and twisted. These are usually "hot."

The large, smooth "cool," or sweet, variety is also called a green, or bell, pepper. Green peppers are widely used in cooking or in fresh salads.

The kind most often used, especially in tropical countries, is the hot *chili*, or red, pepper. The hottest of these small red or yellow fruits is also known as the "bird," or "devil," pepper. In general, the smaller peppers are the hottest.

Indians produced hot sauces and ground pepper by drying the fruits, seeds and all, then grinding them into a fine powder. For thousands of years they used stones for grinding, as some

Indians still do today. The powder was boiled with a liquid to produce a hot sauce that was poured over just about every kind of food. This ancient sauce was similar to Tabasco sauce.

Indians in southwestern United States made a powder called *chili*, with which they used to season many foods. Chili is popular in many countries today, both north and south of the Rio Grande.

MAPLE SUGAR

When the French settled in Quebec, twelve years before the Pilgrims landed at Plymouth, they soon learned how to make maple syrup from the Algonquins. Samuel de Champlain found the Indians making a thick syrup from the sap of trees in the region that is now Vermont. Indians drank the syrup as a food and as an energy-building medicine.

In early spring, northern woodland Indians held a holiday festival when they tapped rock or sugar maple trees. Hollow reed pipes were inserted into a cut in the tree trunk and the sap ran through the pipes into a wooden trough. Indian women dipped the sap into green birch-bark kettles and hung them over the glowing coals of a low fire. The sap was boiled slowly for several days until it thickened into syrup. The French later traded iron kettles for Indian furs, and the native production of syrup soared. The thickened syrup was poured into a cooling trough and kneaded by Indian women with their hands or stirred with a wooden paddle until it was thick and creamy. The women poured this soft sugar into birch-bark moulds, often in the shape of cones. The maple sugar was then stored to eat as a sweet or to flavor foods such as cornmeal mush.

The Iroquois told a legend of maple syrup. Old Nokomis, grandmother of Hiawatha, was supposed to have shown a tribal

hero, Manabusha, how to tap maple trees. At first the sap
came from the trees in a thick syrup. Manabusha, a friend of all
men, thought it was not good for the people to get syrup so
easily—they wouldn't appreciate it unless they worked hard to
make it. Manabusha climbed to the top of the tallest maple tree
and poured water over it to dilute the sap. He then instructed
his people to chop wood, build a bonfire, fashion bark kettles,
and stir the sap while it slowly boiled, watching it carefully all
the while. Manabusha, good friend that he was, couldn't abide
idle people.

WILD RICE

For hundreds of years wild rice was a basic Indian food along
the shores of the Great Lakes. The Chippewas, in the Lake Superior area, were fortunate to have the largest natural fields.
The stems or reeds of wild rice grow close together at the edge
of lakes in water that is several feet deep. Only recently has
"wild" rice been planted successfully in places where it had
never grown before.

The slender stems of wild rice often grow twice as tall as a
man. The grain forms in delicate plumes at the top. Just before
the rice ripens, Indians glide through the fields in canoes. They
pull the stems over gently, tying them into small bundles with
the plumes looped under. This keeps the birds from eating the
ripe grain, and the wind and rain from breaking it off before
harvest.

Harvest was—and is—a time of feasting and dancing, a joyous
thank-you to the Great Spirit who sends the sun and water and
seed for each rice crop.

Men and women still harvest wild rice in the birch-bark canoes that the Chippewas make so well. The man may pole the

canoe through the dense rice field while the woman unties the bundles and whacks them with a stick to beat off the grain. Most of the rice falls into the canoe, but some falls into the water and seeds the fields for another season.

When the canoe is loaded with rice, the harvesters join others of the tribe on shore in a ceremonial hulling of the grain.

The rice is poured into big tubs or troughs that are sunk in the ground. A long pole is hung at hand-height above the tubs, so men can hang on to it while they trampled the grain with their feet, in time to the beat of drums. After a feast of the boiled brown rice and meat, the Indians bag and store the remainder for winter use.

Wild rice is still harvested by hand by the Indians of the Great Lakes area. It is a delicacy that is most often used with turkey or wild game. The supply is limited and it is expensive, probably the most expensive Indian food for its size.

MANIOC OR CASSAVA

Many food plants that were cultivated by the ancient South American Indians never reached North America. Raw manioc, or cassava, is one. This plant grows best in the tropics. Only a few feet high, it has an unusually large root that is often nine inches thick and three feet long, and weighs up to thirty pounds. The cassava root is poisonous.

The plant deserves special mention—as a food, not as a poison. Resourceful tropical Indians learned to remove the prussic acid poison from the root, and to use the remaining product as one of their most important foods.

Tapioca, used both as a pudding and as a thickener, is made from the manioc plant. The plant's boiled-down juice also serves as a basic ingredient for Worcestershire and other sauces.

VANILLA

The vanilla flavoring in cakes, cookies, ice cream, and many other products comes from an orchid plant that grows wild in Mexico and Central and South America. This orchid is valuable for its long, thin bean pod rather than its beautiful flowers.

Most vanilla comes from the lowlands of Eastern Mexico. The plant roots in the ground but climbs for hundreds of feet over large trees. Bees and other insects pollinate the small flowers. Only in this area of Mexico do bees pollinate this flower; in every other place in the world where vanilla is cultivated, men pollinate the plant by hand, flower by flower. It takes one man a whole day to pollinate two hundred blossoms.

About a year after the thin, string-like vanilla pods, or "beans," begin to grow, they are ready for harvest. The beans are cured by a complex fermenting process which the Indians developed thousands of years ago. This food process was both clever and difficult, as creative as the preparation of the seeds of the cacao tree into chocolate and cocoa. Vanilla and chocolate by themselves are rather flavorless, yet each was developed into a delicious drink, proving perhaps that Indian cooks were as talented as Indian farmers!

AVOCADO

Incan, Mayan, and Aztec Indians cultivated avocado trees, which originally grew wild. Avocados are now grown in semi-tropical parts of the United States—Florida, California, Texas, and Hawaii.

The most common fruits are pear-shaped and dark green in color. They vary in weight from half a pound to three or four pounds. The fruit may grow to the size of a large cantaloupe.

Avocados are eaten fresh in salads or as a dip, such as *guaca-mole*, which is made from chopped hot peppers, onions, toma-toes, and mashed avocados.

SQUASH AND PUMPKIN

Squash and pumpkin, which are believed to be the first food plants that were cultivated by Indians, are now grown all over the world. New England Indians called the vines and fruits of both plants *askoot-asquash*. The Pilgrims soon shortened this tongue-twister to "squash."

In many parts of the United States, great orange and yellow piles of squash and pumpkin can be seen at roadside stands in

the autumn, and when the frost is on the pumpkin, northerners know that winter is near. Squash is grown to be baked or mashed or as a filling for pies. Pumpkins are also used in pies. They are also fed to livestock and used as a colorful Halloween decoration, particularly the jack-o'-lantern. Both squash and pumpkin are popular for the traditional Thanksgiving dinner when they are joined by other Indian foods—cranberries, potatoes, sweet potatoes, and, of course, turkey.

The Indians of New England ate squash blossoms fresh, as a salad, or they made soup from them. Sometimes they fried squash in cakes. Always seeking ways to stretch their food supply, Indians used squash and pumpkin seeds, too. They roasted the seeds as nuts, or they pounded dried seeds into powder to make bread-like cakes. Few people would go to that trouble today, but roasted and salted pumpkin seeds enjoy a modest popularity.

JERUSALEM ARTICHOKES

This plant is a sunflower, not the artichoke we eat today. It is often called sunroot and the Indians cultivated the plant for its edible root or tuber. This plant has been largely forgotten, yet it still grows wild from southern Canada into the United States as far south as a line between Washington, D.C. and Omaha, Nebraska. Its less-than-exciting flavor undoubtedly contributed to its neglect.

SUNFLOWER SEEDS

Common sunflowers were cultivated by Indians who lived between the Rocky Mountains and the Atlantic Coast. Sunflowers grew wild in this area and were a hated invader of cornfields.

Through the years, as Indians cultivated and fertilized the plant, sunflower seeds increased greatly in size. Indians dried the seeds and ground them into meal, exactly as they did with corn.

The present cultivated sunflower usually has only one flower that develops into a head that often measures ten inches across. This flower contains thousands of large seeds. These seeds are purchased by many people as food for birds in the winter. Sunflower seed will sprout and grow well in any home garden.

BERRIES

Each growing season the Indians of North America gathered about fifteen kinds of berries to eat fresh or to dry for winter. Blueberries, cranberries, strawberries, raspberries, and blackberries are the best known because they are still cultivated today.

North American cranberries are shipped all over the world, and turkey and cranberries are a natural combination for the traditional American Thanksgiving dinner. Indians pounded blueberries and cranberries into meat, then dried the mixture to make pemmican. Small, flat pemmican cakes kept well for winter use and Indian hunters, trappers, and warriors carried them when they traveled.

Cape Cod cranberry bogs are beautiful in May and June when the little bell-shaped white flowers almost hide the delicate fern-like stems. In September the plant, which is about six inches high, bends over with the weight of the bright red berries. They are delicious when properly cooked as sauce or juice. After the harvest, cranberry foliage turns bronze-red. In winter the bogs are flooded to protect the plants from freezing. Nature is at her dramatic best as the four seasons touch the cranberry bog.

PLUMS

There were about a dozen varieties of wild plums growing in Canada and the United States when the first settlers arrived from Europe. For uncounted years Indians had eaten wild plums fresh and had dried them for winter use. Some wild plums have adapted well to civilization, but most are as wild today as they were when nomadic tribes found them and picked them and then moved on.

The beach plum, that grows only within sniffing distance of salt water, can be found along the Gulf and Atlantic coasts. Beach plums are used to produce delicious—and popular—jellies and jams.

The Canada or wild yellow plum has a delightfully delicate flavor, and the Chickasaw plum still grows wild in the central United States, as far south as Mississippi. Its fruit is reddish-yellow. Larger than other wild plums, its flavor is delicious. Wild Chickasaw plums are plentiful in bottomland thickets along the midwestern creeks in the Mississippi basin. Chickasaws, like beach plums, produce exceptional jams and jellies.

WILD CHERRIES

Chokecherry, wild red cherry, and rum cherry are the best-known of these fruits. The Indians, particularly those in the Plains States, ate them fresh, dried them, and pounded them into wild game to make pemmican.

NUTS

The range of nut-producing trees is many and varied, both in varieties and locales. Indians everywhere found them, and often subsisted on them when other foods were scarce. In both North and South America many different kinds of nut-producing trees and shrubs grew wild. Many of these have been domesticated, but they are virtually the same wild nuts that were harvested and stored by the earliest Indians. Among these are butternuts, black walnuts, pecans, acorns, cashews, chestnuts, filberts, hickory nuts, and *pinon* or pine nuts. Also, there were and are Brazil nuts, which grow only in tropical America. Coconuts, a staple food in many tropical areas, is misnamed, for this "nut" is actually a fruit.

Long years ago, tribes now forgotten discovered that nuts were both delicious and nutritious, but special credit should be given to the Indian who discovered that the husk of the cashew nut was poisonous, but the nut inside was good to eat.

ANIMALS DOMESTICATED OR RAISED FOR FOOD

Early Indian nomads, spreading slowly across the great, vast spaces of North and South America, captured and tamed some of the wild animals they found along the way. Indians domesticated the Inca dog, turkeys, muscovy ducks, guinea pigs, llamas, and alpacas. They encouraged wild bees to swarm and make honey in hives rather than in holes in trees. They hunted and ate wild deer and the buffalo, but these creatures were too numerous, too skittish, or too brutish to tame.

Taming wild llamas and alpacas must have taken considerable skill, but somehow ancient Indian wranglers managed. Both animals are at least as large as deer, and each can outrun a man. America's first colonists, the Indians, didn't have horses until the second wave of immigrants, the Spaniards, moved in, so any fleet-footed llama that was captured must have been by men on foot. It is likely that the first domesticated llamas were captured when they were very young and raised as pets.

The most difficult to explain is the Indian dog. Every Indian tribe, from the earliest wandering families, had their packs of howling, snarling, snapping dogs—mixed breeds of dubious ancestry. It is very possible that the ancestors of these dogs accompanied the earliest nomads on their long trek from Asia, howling, snarling, and snapping every step of the way.

Early explorers, such as de Soto and Lewis and Clark, wrote in their journals about eating delicious roast dog with their Indian hosts. Their descriptions of hunting dogs on the Plains lead some historians to believe that dogs were wild game, related to the coyote, the fox, or the wolf. If so, some of these animals were later raised by the Indians for food, much as Europeans tamed and raised wild pigs. Although "roast dog" didn't refer to the domesticated dogs that guarded Navaho sheep or pulled the Eskimo sled, there is considerable evidence that America's Plains Indians viewed their packs of dogs as fair game, and many a camp-following canine ended up in a cooking pot whenever wild game was scarce. No dogmeat recipes are included in the following section, although one of the most frequently mentioned recipes was a dogmeat stew.

RECIPES ADAPTED FROM INDIAN WAYS OF COOKING

Early Indians used whatever meats and edible plants they found, hunting or gathering some wild, domesticating or cultivating others. Although they had no written recipes, many Indian women were creative cooks. They experimented with the foods at hand, often adding herbs, roots, seeds, or berries as seasoning. The various tribes celebrated special occasions and the passing of the seasons by feasting together. Both foods and recipes were exchanged at these gatherings. These recipes were handed down, mother to daughter, over centuries, and many American favorite foods have been adopted and adapted from these recipes—foods the Indians gave us.

102

Potatoes Baked in Hot Coals

Build a campfire of wood or charcoal well ahead of time so
the fire can die down and leave a deep bed of coals or hot
ashes. Scrub the potatoes, leaving the skin on. Place them in the
hot ashes for about an hour. They are done when a fork or thick

stick will go through the center easily. Split open the hard, blackened crust, and eat the center with butter and salt.

Indian Hash Browns

1 heavy iron or aluminum skillet
3–4 tablespoons of bacon fat, butter or oil

potatoes chopped into small pieces
salt

Melt fat in skillet and salt to taste. Spread potatoes over skillet. Cook layer without turning until crisp and brown on bottom.

Candied Sweet Potatoes

1 cup raw sugar
5 medium boiled sweet potatoes

½ cup water
6 tablespoons butter
salt and pepper to taste

Peel and slice sweet potatoes into a greased baking dish. With sugar and water make a syrup and cook until clear. Add butter and seasoning to syrup, pour over sweet potatoes and bake in a hot oven uncovered for approximately forty-five minutes.

Method of Drying Sweet Potatoes

Wash sweet potatoes and place in kettle of boiling water. Potatoes are cooked when a fork easily pierces skin and meat. When potatoes have cooled, peel and slice. Place slices on clean white cloth and put out in sun each day. When slices have throughly dried they may be stacked and used during winter for puddings, pie, etc.

Roasted Peanuts

Remove skins from raw peanuts.

For each cup of peanuts, heat, in shallow fry pan, four ounces of oil. Only put in enough peanuts at a time to cover bottom of pan and stir until lightly browned. Remove peanuts from pan and drain. When peanuts are well-drained sprinkle with salt and brown in hot oven, stirring occasionally.

Peanut Butter

In wooden chopping bowl put in two cups freshly roasted peanuts. When you have chopped peanuts as fine as possible, take wood spoon or old-fashioned wood potato masher and mash peanuts into consistency of butter.

Modern cooks may not want to take the time to make peanut butter the way the Indians did and for those cooks we suggest they put the freshly roasted peanuts through the kitchen grinder.

Peanut Soup

1 cup peanut butter	¼ cup celery chopped
4 cups milk	2 sprigs parsley
1 cup cold water	1 small bay leaf
1 small onion chopped	salt and pepper
1 tablespoon flour	

Cook onion, celery, bay leaf, and parsley in water until onion and celery are tender. Add peanut butter and milk, bring to boiling point, and simmer about fifteen minutes. Stir often to prevent burning. Mix flour with a little milk and stir in through a sieve. Season to taste and continue to cook and stir until soup is thickened and smooth.

Bean-Hole Beans from Downeast Maine

Prepare an outdoor pit as described in the chapter on beans. The beans can also be baked for ten hours in an oven at 325 degrees.

A two-quart bean pot should be large enough to hold:

2 cups of pea beans, yellow-eyes, red kidney, or limas

½ cup of good molasses

1 rounded teaspoon of dry mustard

2 teaspoons of salt and a dash of pepper

½ pound of salt pork

1 whole peeled onion

Soak the beans overnight in enough cold water to allow for swelling. In the morning drain, then cover again with cold water—about two inches above the beans in the pot. Add the molasses, salt, pepper, and mustard. Bring to a boil. Push the whole onion and the chunk of salt pork down into center of the bean pit. Cover the pot and put it into the bean-hole, as described. If baked in an oven, uncover the beans during last two hours to brown them.

Succotash

2 cups of green beans, shelled

2 cups of raw green corn from cob

salt and pepper

2 tablespoons of butter or

3 tablespoons of thick cream

Cover beans with water and simmer with salt until tender, about forty minutes. While beans are cooking, slice the raw green corn, and scrape off the juice from the cob with a knife. When the beans are done, drain. Heat the corn separately and then add to the beans. Season with salt and pepper to taste. Add butter or thick cream. Bring mixture to a boil and remove from fire at once. Serve for a main course in bowls or in side dishes as a vegetable.

Indians varied succotash by adding bits of meat, such as chipped beef or ham. Others used wild onions, and red and green peppers.

Fried Green Tomatoes

large green tomatoes
2 beaten eggs
1 cup homemade bread-
    crumbs

salt and pepper to taste
2 tablespoons of butter
1 heavy skillet

These taste much like fried eggplant. Slice tomatoes ½ inch thick. Dry the slices. Dip in the eggs, then in breadcrumbs. Salt and pepper. Fry in skillet over moderate fire. They cook quickly.

Green Tomato Pie

5 or 6 large green tomatoes
1 cup raw sugar
2 tablespoons flour

2 tablespoons vinegar
cinnamon
butter

Core and slice tomatoes quite thin, sprinkle lightly with salt, and let stand thirty minutes. Line large pie pan with ordinary piecrust. Put in flour and ½ cup raw sugar. Add tomatoes and then vinegar. Pour remaining sugar over all this. Sprinkle with cinnamon and dot with butter. Add top crust and bake at 400–425 degrees until lightly browned.

Fresh Sweet and Sour Tomatoes

4 ripe tomatoes peeled and cut into bite-size pieces
1 large onion, sliced thin

1 or 2 green sweet peppers, sliced

Mix lightly in a bowl with three tablespoons of vinegar, two tablespoons of new sugar, a quarter teaspoon of salt, and a dash of pepper. Serve in small sauce dishes as a vegetable or salad.

Cocoa and Chocolate

Cacao trees grow in the West Indies, South America, and Mexico. Chocolate and cocoa both come from seeds of the cocoa bean. After roasting, the outer covering of the bean is removed and it is this covering that is known as cocoa shells. The beans are broken and sold as cocoa nibs. Cocoa as we know it on the modern market is made from ground cocoa nibs. Chocolate is also made from cocoa nibs, but contains a much larger proportion of fat than cocoa.

Cocoa Shells

1 cup cocoa shells
6 cups boiling water

pinch of salt

Simmer at least two hours. As water boils away add more water. Strain and serve with milk and raw sugar.

Aztec Chocolate Drink

2 to 3 tablespoons of cocoa   2 tablespoons of raw sugar
Mix cocoa and sugar with one-quarter cup of boiling water. Pour the mixture into a quart of milk and heat, but do not boil, stirring to keep it from burning. Flavor with vanilla bean. Serve hot.

Seafood Chowder or Stew

Seafood chowders or stews are among the easiest foods to experiment with. Choose fresh-caught fish, lobster, crabs, clams, or shrimp, or combinations of these. Cover with hot water and cook until seafood is done—about six to ten minutes for fish, lobster, and crabs or one or two minutes for shrimp and clams. Cool, then remove all meat from the shells or bones. Fresh oysters are not cooked, but should be heated to just below a boil. The simplest stews require only the addition of milk and butter, plus salt and pepper to taste while heating.

Chowders are made by cooking potatoes and onions with salt and pepper until the vegetables are tender, then adding the seafood meat and milk. When they have blended, heat but do not boil.

The Cherokees of Georgia and North and South Carolina combined chicken in a kettle with these vegetables. In season they added fresh wild mushrooms to the stew when it was almost done.

Indian Chicken Stew

young chicken	**½ cup of potatoes**
1 teaspoon of salt	**½ cup of onions**
3 tablespoons of butter	**½ cup of limas or other shell**
½ cup of corn	**beans**
½ cup of tomatoes	**sprig of fresh dill or tarragon**

Cut chicken into serving pieces. Sprinkle with salt, then brown in butter on all sides in a deep pan. Cover with water and simmer about one hour. Add the corn, tomatoes, potatoes, onions, beans and herbs. Cook twenty minutes longer until the chicken is tender. Remove the chicken from the pot, and the meat from the bones. Return meat to the stew, salt, and reheat.

Corn Stew

Many Indian tribes combined foods in a kettle and stewed them in water over a slow fire. They used wild onions and herbs for flavoring. For instance, the Sioux and other Indians on the Plains stewed deer, buffalo, or rabbit meat with potatoes and corn. The fresh corn was cut from the cob and added after the meat was tender, or about ten to fifteen minutes before serving.

From Maine to Massachusetts, coastal Indians made a lobster and corn stew. Along the coast of Maryland, Indians used crab. Gulf Coast Indians used shrimp. Indians of the Pacific coast and rivers made salmon and corn soup.

Fresh Corn Pudding

2 cups fresh corn kernels (about 5 ears)
3 beaten eggs
4 tablespoons of flour
1 teaspoon of salt

1 tablespoon of raw sugar
dash of pepper and nutmeg
2 tablespoons of melted butter
2 cups of milk (or milk and cream)

Stir first seven ingredients. Add the butter and the milk. Bake in a casserole dish set in a pan of water in a 325-degree oven for one hour, or until the top of the pudding is firm like a custard.

Corn Chowder

2 cups corn cut off cob
2 small onions, minced
3–4 cups cubed raw potatoes
1 slice salt pork, diced

2 cups boiling water
3–4 cups scalded milk
2 tablespoons butter
salt and pepper to taste

Fry salt pork until well done. Add onion and cook until transparent, about four to five minutes. Add potatoes and water, and continue cooking until potatoes are soft. Add corn and scalded milk, and heat. This last step is important—just heat but do not boil. Add butter and seasonings and serve.

Corn Fritters

2 cups pulp scraped from fresh, tender corn
3 eggs, well beaten

3 to 4 tablespoons flour
2 tablespoons cream
1 teaspoon salt

One of the best ways to remove pulp from corn on the cob is to draw a sharp knife through each row of corn lengthwise, then scrape pulp out with back of knife.

Beat eggs thoroughly and gradually add corn pulp, beating energetically. Add cream and seasonings and stir in flour, just enough to hold mixture together. Drop by spoonfuls into hot fat and cook until light brown.

This mixture may also be considered a batter and as such may be cooked on a griddle as you would pancakes.

Iroquois Leaf Bread

Scrape green corn from cob, beat into a paste, season with salt and pepper, shape into rolls 3½″ to 4½″ and at least 1½″ in diameter. Wrap this rolled mixture in corn husks, drop in boiling water, and cook approximately forty-five minutes.

To the Mexicans this is known as a Corn Tamale and demonstrates the cooking ties between the North American Indians and the Mexicans.

This Leaf Bread or Corn Tamale may be steamed instead of boiled. Spread with butter or bacon drippings after removing the corn husk wrapper.

Osage Indian Bread

1 tablespoon melted lard
2 cups flour
1½ cups cold water

2 teaspoons baking powder
1 teaspoon salt

Make a dough from above ingredients and roll dough into thin sheet. Cut dough into squares approximately 4" x 4". Cut holes in squares with fork, and drop squares of dough into hot fat. Turn over until both sides are golden brown and well done.

Indian Cake

4 **cups sifted cornmeal**
3 **tablespoons of molasses**
2 **teaspoons of salt**

rounded tablespoon of shortening such as lard or butter

Mix ingredients and add boiling water until mixture is well moistened. Put into a well-greased baking pan, smooth surface with a spoon and bake in hot oven until well browned.

Indian Pudding

1 **quart of milk**
¼ **cup of water**
½ **cup of molasses**
½ **cup stone-ground cornmeal (use *only* stoneground)**

1 **tablespoon of butter**
2 **tablespoons of sugar**
½ **teaspoon of salt**
¼ **teaspoon each of nutmeg, ginger, and cinnamon**
1 **beaten egg**

Scald the milk. Mix the water, molasses and cornmeal. Blend this mixture into milk and boil. Remove from the fire and add butter, sugar, salt, and the other seasonings. Cool (it does not have to be cold, only cooler) and add egg. Bake one hour at 325 degrees in casserole or baking dish.